LIBERTY

Funding for this highly-acclaimed Primer on American Liberty, "endowed by [our] Creator" and codified by our Founders in the Declaration of Independence and the U.S. Constitution, is provided in part, by *The Patriot Post* and The Essential Liberty Project.

The Patriot's Primer on American Liberty (first published as "Essential Liberty") has a proven record as an essential scholastic resource for Patriots of all ages. It includes a comprehensive introduction to American Liberty by Mark Alexander, summarizing the eternal struggle between Liberty and tyranny – the primacy of Rule of Law over rule of men, essential to sustain American Liberty.

These Primers on American Liberty may be purchased and/or sponsored for bulk distribution to students, grassroots organizations, civic clubs, military and public service personnel, professional associations and other groups. The Primer covers may also be customized at the discretion of Publius Press, Inc., for special group distributions. To obtain additional copies of "The Patriot's Primer on American Liberty" and our companion booklet, "Founders' Wisdom," visit PatriotPostShop.US.

"We hold these truths to be self-evident, that all men are created equal, that they are endowed by their Creator with certain unalienable Rights, that among these are Life, Liberty and the pursuit of Happiness. ... And for the support of this Declaration, with a firm reliance on the protection of divine Providence, we mutually pledge to each other our Lives, our Fortunes and our sacred Honor."
—The Founders, Declaration of Independence

The Patriot's Primer on American Liberty
was written, designed and produced in the USA.

ACCLAIM FOR THE PATRIOT POST

Harvard Political Review: "*The Patriot Post* is leading a surprisingly well-organized charge into the world of Internet politics."

Michael Reagan, Author and Political Commentator: "The vision and legacy of the Reagan Revolution flourish on the pages of *The Patriot Post*."

Walter E. Williams, Economist: "*The Patriot Post* does a yeoman's job advocating for the moral superiority of personal Liberty and its key ingredient, limited government, as specified by our Founders."

Bill Bennett, Author and Historian: "*The Patriot Post* is leading the charge in the battle to restore America's values — a vital ally on the front...."

Newt Gingrich, Former House Majority Leader: "*The Patriot Post* gets it right, with clarity and consistency!"

Dick Armey, Former House Majority Leader: "Simply put, *The Patriot Post* cuts through the clutter and delivers timely, accurate, and colorful accounts of the week's most important news and policy issues. It's a mandatory read."

Edwin Feulner, Heritage Foundation President: "The best Websites wield remarkable influence in the marketplace of ideas. *The Patriot Post* is a 'must read' for informed conservatives."

Larry Arnn, Constitutional Scholar: "Daniel Webster was right, 'God grants liberty only to those who love it and are always ready to guard and defend it.' *Patriot Post* readers understand that commission."

Senator Rand Paul: "*The Patriot Post* provides a clear and substantial voice for America's Constitutional Conservatives."

Cal Thomas, Author and Political Commentator: "*The Patriot Post* interprets current issues in the conservative context of history."

LtGen, U.S. Marine Corps: "The unapologetic affirmation of Liberty in every edition of *The Patriot Post* is a touchstone for our Marines."

VADM, U.S. Navy: "*The Patriot Post* reaches out to our sailors, especially those serving far away and in harm's way, affirming their service and sacrifice ensuring the flame of Liberty burns bright."

LTG, U.S. Army: "*The Patriot Post* is read by soldiers around the world, and its timeless message of Liberty is an inspiration for our brave war fighters."

Maj. Gen., U.S. Air Force: "Our nation's legacy of Liberty shines through in every edition of *The Patriot Post*!"

TABLE OF CONTENTS

THE PATRIOT'S PRIMER ON AMERICAN LIBERTY
A TREATISE ON THE ETERNAL STRUGGLE BETWEEN LIBERTY AND TYRANNY, AND ON THE PRIMACY OF RULE OF LAW OVER RULE OF MEN

MARK ALEXANDER
PUBLISHER OF THE PATRIOT POST

"Our cause is noble; it is the cause of mankind!"
—*George Washington*

Sons of Liberty — The Fight for Freedom

"The tree of Liberty must be refreshed from time to time with the blood of patriots and tyrants." —*Thomas Jefferson*

On December 16th, 1773, "radicals" in Boston, members of a secret organization of American Patriots called Sons of Liberty, boarded three East India Company ships at Griffin's Wharf and threw 342 chests of British East India Company tea into Boston Harbor. This iconic event, which foretold the revolution to come against oppressive taxation and tyrannical rule, is immortalized as "The Boston Tea Party."

Resistance to the British Crown had been mounting since King George imposed the Writs of Assistance, giving British authorities power to arrest and detain colonists for any reason. He also imposed oppressive bills of attainder and authorized troops to "quarter" in the homes of his colonial subjects. Protests intensified over enactment of heavy taxes, including the 1764 Sugar Act, 1765 Stamp Act and 1767 Townshend Acts.

The growing unrest came to bloodshed in March of 1770, when British troops fired on civilians in Boston, killing five colonists. This event, the "Boston Massacre," gave rise to the slogan, "No taxation without representation."

But it was the 1773 Tea Act, under which the Crown collected a three-pence tax on each pound of tea imported to the colonies, that instigated many Tea Party protests and seeded the American Revolution. Indeed, as James Madison reflected in 1823, "The people of the U.S. owe their Independence and their Liberty, to the wisdom of descrying in the minute tax of 3 pence on tea, the magnitude of the evil comprised in the precedent."

News of the Tea Party protest in Boston galvanized the colonial movement opposing onerous British parliamentary acts that were a violation of the natural, charter and constitutional rights of the British colonists.

In response to the rising colonial unrest, the British enacted measures to punish the citizens of Massachusetts and to reverse the trend of resistance to the Crown's authority. These were labeled "The Intolerable Acts," the first of which was the 1774 Boston Port Bill that blockaded the harbor in an effort to starve Bostonians into submission.

Among the Patriots who broke the blockade to supply food to the people of Boston was William Prescott, who would later prove himself a heroic military leader at Bunker Hill and Saratoga. To his fellow Patriots in Boston, Prescott wrote, "We heartily sympathize with you, and are always ready to do all in our power for your support, comfort and relief; knowing that Providence has placed you where you must stand the first shock. ... Our forefathers passed the vast Atlantic, spent their blood and treasure, that they might enjoy their liberties, both civil and religious, and transmit them to their posterity. ... Now if we should give them up, can our children rise up and call us blessed?"

The Boston blockade was followed by the Massachusetts Government Act, the Administration of Justice Act and the Quartering Act. But far from accomplishing their desired outcome, the Crown's oppressive countermeasures hardened colonial resistance and led to the convention of the First Continental Congress on September 5th, 1774, in Philadelphia.

By March of 1775, civil discontent was at its tipping point, and American Patriots in Massachusetts and other colonies were preparing to cast off their masters. The spirit of the coming Revolution was captured in Patrick Henry's impassioned "Give me Liberty or give me death" speech.

That month, Dr. Joseph Warren delivered a fiery oration in Boston, warning of complacency and instilling courage among his fellow Patriots: "The man who meanly will submit to wear a shackle, contemns the noblest gift of heaven, and impiously affronts the God that made him free. ... Ease and prosperity (though pleasing for a day) have often sunk a people into effeminacy and sloth. ... Our country is in danger, but not to be despaired of. Our enemies are numerous and powerful; but we have many friends, determining to be free, and heaven and earth will aid the resolution. On you depend the fortunes of America. You are to decide the important question, on which rest the happiness and liberty of millions yet unborn. Act worthy of yourselves."

On the eve of April 18th, 1775, General Thomas Gage, royal military governor of Massachusetts, dispatched a force of 700 British Army regulars under Lieutenant Colonel Francis Smith with secret orders to arrest Boston Tea Party leader Samuel Adams, Massachusetts Provincial Congress President John Hancock and merchant fleet owner Jeremiah Lee.

But what directly tied Gage's orders to the later enumeration of the Second Amendment in our Constitution was the primary mission of his Redcoats: A preemptive raid to confiscate arms and ammunition stored by Massachusetts Patriots in the town of Concord. The citizen minutemen understood even then that their right to keep and bear arms should not be infringed.

Patriot militia and minutemen, under the leadership of the Sons of Liberty, anticipated this raid, and the confrontations between militia and British regulars at Lexington and Concord were the fuse that ignited the American Revolution.

Near midnight on April 18th, Paul Revere, who had arranged for advance warning of British movements, departed Charlestown (near Boston) for Lexington and Concord in order to warn John Hancock, Samuel Adams and other Sons of Liberty that the British Army was marching to arrest them and seize their weapons caches. After meeting with Hancock and Adams in Lexington, Revere was captured, but his Patriot ally, Samuel Prescott, continued to Concord and warned militiamen along the way.

The Patriots in Lexington and Concord, as with other militia units in New England, were bound by "minit men" oaths to "stand at a minits warning with arms and ammunition." The oath of the Lexington militia read thus: "We trust in God that, Should the state of our affairs require it, We shall be ready to sacrifice our estates and everything dear in life, Yea, and life itself, in support of the common cause."

In the early dawn of April 19th, their oaths would be tested with blood. Under the command of Captain John Parker, 77 militiamen assembled on the town green at Lexington, where they soon faced Smith's overwhelming force of British regulars. Parker did not expect shots to be exchanged, but his orders were: "Stand your ground. Don't fire unless fired upon, but if they mean to have a war, let it begin here."

A few links away from the militia column, British Major John Pitcairn swung his sword and ordered, "Lay down your arms, you damned rebels!"

Not willing to sacrifice his small band of Patriots on the green, as Parker later wrote in sworn deposition, "I immediately ordered our Militia to disperse, and not to fire." But the Patriots did not lay down their arms as ordered, and as Parker noted, "Immediately said Troops made their appearance and rushed furiously, fired upon, and killed eight of our Party without receiving any Provocation therefor from us."

The British continued to Concord, where they divided ranks and searched for armament stores. Later in the day, the second confrontation between regulars and militiamen occurred as British light infantry companies faced rapidly growing ranks of militia and minutemen at Concord's Old North Bridge. From depositions on both sides, the British fired first, killing two and wounding four.

This time, however, the militia commander, Major John Buttrick, yelled the order, "Fire, for God's sake, fellow soldiers, fire!"

And fire they did, commencing with "The Shot Heard Round the World," as immortalized by poet Ralph Waldo Emerson. With that shot, farmers and laborers, landowners and statesmen alike brought upon themselves the sentence of death for treason. In the ensuing firefight, the British suffered heavy casualties and in discord retreated to Concord village proper for reinforcements, and then back toward Lexington.

During that retreat, British regulars took additional casualties, including those suffered in an ambush by the reassembled ranks of John Parker's militia — "Parker's Revenge," as it became known. The English were reinforced with 1,000 troops in Lexington, but the King's men were no match for the militiamen, who inflicted heavy casualties upon the Redcoats along their 20-mile tactical retreat to Boston.

"What a glorious morning this is!" declared Samuel Adams to fellow Patriot John Hancock upon hearing those first shots.

Indeed, the first shots of the eight-year struggle for American independence were in direct response to the government's attempt to disarm the people.

Thus began the American Revolution — a revolution in support of Liberty not just for the people of Massachusetts but for "all people." Such rights are not temporal, they are eternal.

By the time the Second Continental Congress convened in the Spring of 1775, the young nation was in open war for Liberty and independence, which would not be won until nearly a decade later, at great cost of blood and treasure.

In January of 1776, Thomas Paine published his pamphlet *Common Sense*, which framed the uprising, noting, "The cause of America is in a great measure the cause of all mankind."

Of the justification for Revolution, Samuel Adams wrote, "The People alone have an incontestable, unalienable, and indefeasible right to institute government and to reform, alter, or totally change the same when their protection, safety, prosperity, and happiness require it."

On May 15th of 1776, the Continental Congress adopted a resolution calling on states to prepare for rebellion. In its preamble, John Adams advised his countrymen to sever all oaths of allegiance to the Crown.

"Endowed by Their Creator"

*"In the supposed state of nature, all men are equally
bound by the laws of nature, or to speak more properly,
the laws of the Creator." —Samuel Adams*

On July 2nd, 1776, delegations from the 13 sovereign states, in convention as the Second Continental Congress at the Pennsylvania State House, voted in support of a much-debated resolution for unity and independence. There was one abstention from the New York delegation, which had not yet received permission from its Provincial Congress to vote in the affirmative.

On July 3rd, John Adams wrote his wife Abigail: "Yesterday, the greatest question was decided, which ever was debated in America, and a greater, perhaps, never was or will be decided among men. ... You will see in a few days a Declaration setting forth the causes which have impelled us to this mighty revolution, and the reasons which will justify it in the sight of God and man."

Adams continued: "The Second Day of July 1776, will be the most memorable Epocha, in the History of America. I am apt to believe that it will be celebrated, by succeeding Generations, as the great anniversary Festival. It ought to be commemorated, as the Day of Deliverance by solemn Acts of Devotion to God Almighty. It ought to be solemnized with Pomp and Parade, with Shews, Games, Sports, Guns, Bells, Bonfires and Illuminations from one End of this Continent to the other from this Time forward forever more. You will think me transported with Enthusiasm but I am not. I am well aware of the Toil and Blood and Treasure, that it will cost Us to maintain this Declaration, and support and defend these States. Yet through all the Gloom I can see the Rays of ravishing Light and Glory."

He concluded, "I can see that the End is more than worth all the Means. And that Posterity will tryumph in that Day's Transaction, even altho We should rue it, which I trust in God We shall not."

The delegates then spent two days reviewing the draft of the proposed declaration for independence, which John Adams had requested Thomas Jefferson compose. After revisions and deletions, it was ratified on July 4th and signed by John Hancock, president of the Continental Congress. July 4th has since become the Independence Day we celebrate with "Pomp and Parade, with Shews, Games, Sports, Guns, Bells, Bonfires and Illuminations."

On the night of its enactment, printer John Dunlap produced the first 200 broadsides for distribution. Notably, however, the famous parchment copy of the Declaration now in the National Archives was ordered by Congress on July 19th — including the additional word "unanimous" after the New York delegation affirmed its support. It was then signed by 56 Patriots, some of whom were not present in

Philadelphia in early July. Most signed in early August, with the last signature affixed on November 4th.

The delegate signers were merchants, farmers, doctors, lawyers and others, all of whom pledged "our lives, our fortunes and our sacred honor" to the cause of Liberty. And nine of the 56 did lose their lives in the ensuing conflict.

They declared, "When in the Course of human events, it becomes necessary for one people to dissolve the political bands which have connected them with another, and to assume among the powers of the earth, the separate and equal station to which the Laws of Nature and of Nature's God entitle them, a decent respect to the opinions of mankind requires that they should declare the causes which impel them to the separation."

Our Founders further avowed in the Declaration, "We hold these truths to be self-evident, that all men are created equal, that they are endowed by their Creator with certain unalienable Rights, that among these are Life, Liberty and the pursuit of Happiness. That to secure these rights, Governments are instituted among Men, deriving their just powers from the consent of the governed, That whenever any Form of Government becomes destructive of these ends, it is the Right of the People to alter or to abolish it, and to institute new Government, laying its foundation on such principles and organizing its powers in such form, as to them shall seem most likely to effect their Safety and Happiness."

Our Declaration of Independence was derived from common law, "the Laws of Nature and Nature's God." And the assertion that the rights of all men were irrevocable as "endowed by their Creator" rather than by kings and magistrates was radical, as was its call upon "the Supreme Judge of the world" for "protection of Divine Providence."

The Declaration's first paragraph references "the separate and equal station to which the Laws of Nature and of Nature's God entitle them," which informs the words "endowed by their Creator" in the second paragraph.

To better understand what is meant by "the Laws of Nature and of Nature's God," recall that our Declaration's signers were not of one mind on matters of theology and doctrine. They were Christians, Deists and Agnostics, but they did, however, uniformly declare that the Rights of all people were, are and forever will be innate and unalienable, as established by "the Laws of Nature and of Nature's God." (Notably, references to God and our Creator are also carried through all 50 state constitutions.)

This is not an article of "faith." It is the assertion that the right to "Life, Liberty and the pursuit of Happiness," as enshrined in our Declaration, is inherent and applicable to all humans of every nation, religion, race and ethnicity, and for all time.

It makes no difference what one's concept of "Nature's God" or our "Creator" is, or whether one even subscribes to any such understanding. All people are entitled to Liberty and all the rights so embodied. Those rights are not the gift of man nor the declarations and constitutions written by men. As Founder Alexander Hamilton wrote, "The sacred Rights of mankind are not to be rummaged for among old parchments or musty records. They are written, as with a sun beam, in the whole volume of human nature, by the Hand of the Divinity itself, and can never be erased or obscured by mortal power." Indeed, the Declaration and Constitution were designed specifically to protect those rights, not award them.

"Life, Liberty and the pursuit of Happiness..." These are natural rights — gifts from God, not government.

The Declaration's common law inspiration for the Rights of Man has its origin in governing documents dating back to the 1164 English Constitutions of Clarendon and 1215 Magna Carta. Each established objective Rule of Law over and above the subjective rule of the king. Rex Lex ("The king is law") was slowly replaced by Lex Rex ("The law is king"). With the Magna Carta, the king was bound under the law by a national covenant — a declaration of mutual obligations of the ruler and those ruled.

In his 1690 *Second Treatise on Government*, John Locke articulated this contractual vision of a government of laws existing to protect the liberties of its citizens. The context for Locke's thought was the Glorious Revolution (1688) and the English Bill of Rights (1689).

However, our Declaration's most contemporary common law inspiration was William Blackstone's 1765 *Commentaries on the Laws of England*, perhaps the most scholarly historic and analytic treatise on Natural Law.

Blackstone wrote, "As man depends absolutely upon his Maker for everything, it is necessary that he should in all points conform to his Maker's will. This will of his Maker is called the law of nature. ... This law of nature, being coeval [coexistent] with mankind and dictated by God Himself, is, of course, superior in obligation to any other. It is binding over all the globe, in all countries, and at all times; no human laws are of any validity if contrary to this. ... Upon these two foundations, the law of nature and the law of revelation, depend all human laws; that is to say, no human laws should be suffered [permitted] to contradict these."

Justice James Wilson, a signer of both the Declaration of Independence and the Constitution, and one of George Washington's first nominees to the Supreme Court, wrote, "Law ... communicated to us by reason and conscience ... has been called natural; as promulgated by the Holy Scriptures, it has been called revealed. ... But it should always be remembered, that this law, natural or revealed ... flows from the same divine source; it is the law of God. ... Human law must rest its authority, ultimately, upon the authority of that law, which is divine."

As John Adams resolved, "If men through fear, fraud or mistake, should in terms renounce and give up any essential natural right, the eternal law of reason and the great end of society, would absolutely vacate such renunciation; the right to freedom being the gift of God Almighty, it is not in the power of Man to alienate this gift, and voluntarily become a slave."

It is these fundamental principles of Liberty, as "endowed" and protected by Rule of Law, that Thomas Jefferson enumerated in our Declaration of Independence, and which James Madison later codified in our Constitution.

"We Resolve to Conquer or Die"

"The fate of unborn millions will now depend, under God, on the courage and conduct of this army. ... We have therefore to resolve to conquer or die: Our own Country's Honor, all call upon us for a vigorous and manly exertion, and if we now shamefully fail, we shall become infamous to the whole world." —George Washington

On July 6th, 1776, Congress approved the "Declaration of the Cause and Necessity of Taking up Arms," drafted by Thomas Jefferson and John Dickinson, which noted: "With hearts fortified with these animating reflections, we most solemnly, before God and the world, declare, that, exerting the utmost energy of those powers, which our beneficent Creator hath graciously bestowed upon us, the arms we have been compelled by our enemies to assume, we will, in defiance of every hazard, with unabating firmness and perseverance employ for the preservation of our liberties; being with one mind resolved to die freemen rather than to live as slaves."

At the advent of the American Revolution, John Adams wrote, "Objects of the most stupendous magnitude, and measure in which the lives and liberties of millions yet unborn are intimately interested, are now before us. We are in the very midst of a revolution the most complete, unexpected and remarkable of any in the history of nations."

Samuel Adams captured the spirit of the Revolution in his state-house speech in Philadelphia a month after the Declaration's signing: "Courage, then, my countrymen; our contest is not only whether we ourselves shall be free, but whether there shall be left to mankind an asylum on earth for civil and religious Liberty. ... If I have a wish dearer to my soul than that my ashes may be mingled with those of a Warren and Montgomery, it is that these American States may never cease to be free and independent."

In December of 1776, Thomas Paine wrote in *The American Crisis* of the contest for Liberty: "These are the times that try men's souls. The summer soldier and the sunshine patriot will, in this crisis, shrink from the service of their country; but he that stands by it now, deserves the love and thanks of man and woman. Tyranny, like hell, is not easily conquered; yet we have this consolation with us, that the harder the conflict, the more glorious the triumph. What we obtain too cheap, we esteem too lightly. ... Heaven knows how to put a price upon its goods; and it would be strange indeed if so celestial an article as freedom should not be highly rated..."

As Benjamin Franklin noted, "It is a common observation here that our cause is the cause of all mankind, and that we are fighting for their Liberty in defending our own."

American Patriots faced what seemed to be insurmountable odds, but their leader, George Washington, who was unanimously chosen as Commander in Chief of the Continental Army, was both a proven and Divinely inspired military leader.

Washington had proven his steadfast leadership as a Virginia militia officer in the French and Indian War two decades before the Revolution, most notably at the Battle of the Monongahela. When the French and their Indian allies ambushed General Edward Braddock's forces and mortally wounded Braddock, the British were retreating in chaos. But Washington rode back and forth amid the pitched battle, rallying the Redcoats and his Virginians into an ordered retreat. In the process, two horses were shot from under him, and he would later count four bullet holes through his coat.

Concerning overwhelming odds, Washington wrote in his General Orders of 1776, "Let us therefore rely upon the goodness of the Cause, and the aid of the supreme Being, in whose hands victory is, to animate and encourage us to great and noble Actions — The Eyes of all our Countrymen are now upon us, and we shall have their blessings, and praises, if happily we are the instruments of saving them from the Tyranny mediated against them. Let us therefore animate and encourage each other, and shew the whole world, that a Freeman contending for Liberty on his own ground is superior to any slavish mercenary on earth.

Washington continued, "The hour is fast approaching, on which the Honor and Success of this army, and the safety of our bleeding Country depend. Remember officers and Soldiers, that you are Freemen, fighting for the blessings of Liberty — that slavery will be your portion, and that of your posterity, if you do not acquit yourselves like men."

The Revolutionary War was hard fought and nearly lost on many fields. There were pitched and bloody battles between the onset at Lexington/Concord in 1775 and the war's conclusion with the Treaty of Paris in 1783. The most notable of those battles were Ticonderoga (May 1775), Bunker Hill (June 1775), Quebec (December 1775), Charleston (June 1776), Trenton (December 1776), Bennington (August 1777), Saratoga (October 1777), the encampment at Valley Forge (December 1777), Monmouth (June 1778), Rhode Island (August 1778), Kings Mountain (October 1780), Cowpens (January 1781) and finally Yorktown (October 1781).

There were some 6,800 American battle deaths, with overall deaths including starvation and disease of more than 55,000. Our French ally suffered more than 10,000 battle deaths (most at sea) and their Spanish ally bore more than 5,000 casualties. By comparison with the casualty counts of the 20th century's world wars, these are small, but the population of the 13 colonies in 1776 was just 2.3 million, less than 15 percent of the population of Britain at the time.

At war's end in 1783, Washington wrote, "It is yet to be decided whether the revolution must ultimately be considered as a blessing or a curse: a blessing or a curse, not to the present age alone, for with our fate will the destiny of unborn millions be involved."

Benjamin Rush observed, "The American war is over; but this far from being the case with the American revolution. On the contrary, nothing but the first act of the drama is closed. It remains yet to establish and perfect our new forms of government, and to prepare the principles, morals, and manners of our citizens for these forms of government after they are established and brought to perfection."

In retrospect, John Adams wrote, "But what do we mean by the American Revolution? Do we mean the American war? The revolution was effected before the war commenced. The revolution was in the minds and hearts of the People; a change in their religious sentiments, of their duties and obligations. ... This radical change in the principles, opinions, sentiments, and affections of the People was the real American revolution."

Rather than anoint himself king, as some speculated he might, General Washington chose instead to return to his Mount Vernon farm. When King George III heard from his American-born portrait painter, Benjamin West, that Washington would retire rather than take power, he replied, "If he does that, he will be the greatest man in the world."

Fortunately, Washington was later persuaded to return to public service as our nation's first president. The man also known as the Father of our Country and its "Indispensable Man" set a lasting standard for presidential character.

"We the People"

*"We the People of the United States, in Order to form
a more perfect Union, establish Justice, insure domestic Tranquility, provide for the common defence, promote the general Welfare,
and secure the Blessings of Liberty to ourselves and our Posterity,
do ordain and establish this Constitution for the United States of
America." —Preamble to the Constitution of the United States*

In 1776, the Second Continental Congress appointed a committee
representing the 13 newly sovreign states to draft a formal document
of incorporation. On November 15th, 1777, the states approved the
Articles of Confederation and Perpetual Union. The Articles, which
maintained the maximal autonomy of the individual states, were finally ratified on March 1st, 1781, and "the United States in Congress
assembled" became the Congress of the Confederation.

Returning focus to the issue of self-governance at the close of
the Revolutionary War, it was evident to most American leaders that
the Articles of Confederation between the states did not sufficiently
ensure the interests and security of the Confederation. In September
of 1786, at the urging of James Madison, 12 delegates from five states
(New Jersey, New York, Pennsylvania, Delaware and Virginia) met in
Annapolis, Maryland, to consider amendments to the Articles.

Those delegates called for representatives from every state to
convene at the Pennsylvania State House in Philadelphia for full
consideration of the revisions needed, and 12 states (Rhode Island
declining) sent 55 delegates, a third of whom had signed the Declaration of Independence.

The most noted delegates were George Washington, James Madi-
son, Roger Sherman, Alexander Hamilton, Benjamin Franklin and
George Mason. (Thomas Jefferson was in Europe in his capacity as
Minister to France, but he expressed his cautious support for the new
Constitution in correspondence with Madison.)

Noticeably absent from the proceedings were Patrick Henry,
Samuel Adams and Thomas Paine, who believed the Articles did not
need replacement, only modification. They were concerned that a
proceeding aimed at establishing a new constitution could imperil our
fundamental liberties. Summing up their sentiments, Henry wrote that
he "smelt a rat in Philadelphia, tending toward the monarchy."

The Philadelphia (Constitutional) Convention opened its proceedings on May 25th, 1787, having unanimously chosen George Washington as convention president, and soon decided against amending
the existing Articles in favor of drafting a new constitution. The next
three months were devoted to deliberations on various proposals with
the objective of drafting a document that would secure the rights and
principles enumerated in the Declaration of Independence and in the

11

Articles of Confederation, thus preserving Liberty.

In late July, after much debate, a Committee of Detail was appointed to draft a document to include all of the compromise agreements, but based primarily on Madison's Virginia Plan, establishing a republican form of government subject to strict Rule of Law, reflecting the consent of the people and severely limiting the power of the central government.

A month later, the Committee of Style and Arrangement, which included James Madison as primary author and intellectual inspiration, Gouverneur Morris, Alexander Hamilton, William Samuel Johnson and Rufus King, produced the final draft of the Constitution, which was then submitted September 17th, 1787, for delegate signatures. Here it must be stressed that this document established a republic, not a popular democracy — which is to say that it affirmed the primacy of Rule of Law over the rule of men.

Said Benjamin Franklin of the new document, "I confess that there are several parts of this constitution which I do not at present approve, but I am not sure I shall never approve them: For having lived long, I have experienced many instances of being obliged by better information, or fuller consideration, to change opinions even on important subjects, which I once thought right, but found to be otherwise. ... Thus I consent, Sir, to this Constitution because I expect no better, and because I am not sure, that it is not the best."

Of the 55 delegates, 39 signed the new Constitution while the remaining delegates declined, most out of concern that the power apportioned through the new plan was a threat to the sovereignty of the several states and, thus, to individual Liberty.

The ensuing ratification debates among the states were vigorous. James Madison, John Jay and Alexander Hamilton authored *The Federalist Papers*, which advocated ratification of the new Constitution and the strong central government it established. *The Federalist Papers* remain to this day its most detailed explication — affirming the original meaning and intent of our nation's founding document.

Patrick Henry's Anti-Federalists opposed the plan under consideration because they believed it allocated too much power to the central government. Henry, Samuel Adams, George Mason, Robert Yates, Thomas Paine, Samuel Bryan and Richard Henry Lee were among those who spoke against ratification, and some authored several essays that were aggregated and published as *The Anti-Federalist Papers*.

The Federalists prevailed, but Madison conceded, "It has been said that all Government is an evil. It would be more proper to say that the necessity of any Government is a misfortune. This necessity however exists; and the problem to be solved is, not what form of

Government is perfect, but which of the forms is least imperfect."

To that end, it is important to note that the "strong central government" established by our Constitution bore no resemblance to, nor did that document authorize, the behemoth, intrusive, statist central government of today.

In Federalist No. 32, Hamilton notes, "But as the plan of the [Constitutional] convention aims only at a partial union or consolidation, the State governments would clearly retain all the rights of sovereignty which they before had, and which were not, by that act, exclusively delegated to the United States."

The new Constitution stipulated that once nine of the 13 original states ratified it through state conventions, a date would be established for its implementation. This created controversy, as the document in question had no standing authority to make such a stipulation. However, once the ninth state, New Hampshire, reported its convention's approval on June 21st, 1788, the Continental Congress set the date for enactment of the Constitution for March 4th, 1789.

With Rhode Island's ratification on May 29th, 1790, all 13 states endorsed the Constitution.

Though critical of many of its provisions, Thomas Jefferson wrote in reflection of the Convention and its product, "The example of changing a constitution by assembling the wise men of the state, instead of assembling armies, will be worth as much to the world as the former examples we had given them. The constitution, too, which was the result of our deliberation, is unquestionably the wisest ever yet presented to men."

Our Founders affirmed that the natural rights enumerated in our Declaration of Independence and, by extension, as codified in its subordinate guidance, our Constitution, are those endowed by our Creator. Regarding the supremacy of the Declaration's enumerations, on the occasion of the Declaration's 50th anniversary, Madison wrote to Jefferson, "On the distinctive principles of the Government ... of the U. States, the best guides are to be found in ... The Declaration of Independence, as the fundamental Act of Union of these States."

Hence, the Articles of Confederation and its successor, the U.S. Constitution, were created as contractual agreements binding the several states into one strong union in defense of Liberty as our national motto implies — E Pluribus Unum. But the innate Rights of Man identified in the Declaration are the overarching basis of that union, irrevocable and non-negotiable by way of "collective agreement and compromise."

James Madison observed, "It is impossible for the man of pious reflection not to perceive in [the Constitution] a finger of that Almighty hand which has been so frequently and signally extended to our relief in the critical stages of the revolution."

George Washington was unanimously elected by the Electoral College twice, after national elections in 1789 and 1792, and served our new nation until 1797, when he chose, once again, to return to his Mount Vernon farm.

"To Secure These Rights"

"In order to prevent misconstruction or abuse
of [the Constitution's] powers..." —Preamble to the Bill of Rights

Endeavoring to further define our Constitution's limits on governmental encroachment upon the innate rights of the people, James Madison, its primary architect, introduced to the First Congress in 1789 a Bill of Rights — which was ratified on December 15th, 1791.

The Bill of Rights was inspired by three remarkable documents: Two Treatises of Government, authored by John Locke in 1689 regarding protection of "property" (in the Latin context, *proprius*, or one's own "life, Liberty and estate"); the Virginia Declaration of Rights, authored by George Mason in 1776 as part of that state's constitution; and, of course, our Declaration of Independence, authored by Thomas Jefferson.

Though the Bill of Rights is commonly referred to as "the first ten amendments" to our Constitution, it is important to distinguish these ten articles from amendments — the former being an integral part of our Constitution, while the latter, over the course of our nation's history, having modified it.

Because of that distinction, the addition of the Bill of Rights was hotly debated among our Founders, many of whom argued that the mere reiteration of these innate and unalienable Rights of Man within the Constitution might imply that they are somehow subject to amendment, as if granted by the state.

Alexander Hamilton argued in Federalist No. 84, "Bills of rights, in the sense and in the extent in which they are contended for, are not only unnecessary in the proposed constitution, but would even be dangerous. They would contain various exceptions to powers which are not granted; and on this very account, would afford a colorable pretext to claim more than were granted. For why declare that things shall not be done which there is no power to do?"

On the other hand, George Mason was among 16 of the 55 Constitutional Convention delegates who refused to sign because the document did not adequately address limitations on what the central government had "no power to do." Indeed, he worked with Patrick Henry and Samuel Adams against its ratification for that very reason.

As a result of Mason's insistence, the first session of Congress incorporated those ten additional limitations upon the federal government for the reasons outlined by the Preamble to the Bill of Rights: "The Conventions of a number of the States having at the time of their adopting the Constitution, expressed a desire, in order to prevent misconstruction or abuse of its powers, that further declaratory and restrictive clauses should be added: And as extending the ground of public confidence in the Government, will best insure the beneficent ends of its institution."

Read in context, the Bill of Rights is both another affirmation of the unalienable Rights of Man as "endowed by their Creator" and a clear proscription upon any central government infringement of those rights. The purpose of its inclusion was, without question, to further secure those rights.

"An Evil of Colossal Magnitude"

Much has rightly been said of the fact that, at the time our Constitution was ratified, many Africans were enslaved on our continent. Notably, the roots of abolition were also established in that same era.

In 1773, Patrick Henry wrote, "I believe a time will come when an opportunity will be offered to abolish this lamentable evil. Everything we do is to improve it, if it happens in our day; if not, let us transmit to our descendants, together with our slaves, a pity for their unhappy lot and an abhorrence of slavery."

A year later, Thomas Jefferson wrote, "The abolition of domestic slavery is the great object of desire in those colonies, where it was unhappily introduced in their infant state."

In his draft of the Declaration, Jefferson wrote, "[King George] has waged cruel war against human nature itself, violating its most sacred rights of life and Liberty in the persons of a distant people who never offended him, captivating & carrying them into slavery in another hemisphere, or to incur miserable death in their transportation thither."

"Negro slavery," said John Adams, "is an evil of colossal magnitude," and Benjamin Franklin concluded that slavery was "an atrocious debasement of human nature."

During the constitutional debates, James Madison observed, "The real difference of interests, lay not between large and small, but between the Northern and Southern states. The institution of slavery and its consequences formed a line of discrimination."

George Washington would later write, "I wish from my soul that the legislature of [Virginia] could see the policy of a gradual Abolition of slavery."

Slaves would not be fully emancipated until the end of the cataclysmic War Between the States that was, ironically, fought over offense to the Constitution's assurance of states' rights. That emancipation was codified in 1865 with the ratification of the Thirteenth Amendment.

Rule of Law

"They define a republic to be a government of laws, and not of men."
—*John Adams*

Article VI of our Constitution proclaims: "This Constitution ... shall be the supreme Law of the Land."

For its first 150 years (with a few exceptions), our Constitution and Rule of Law stood mostly as our Founders and "The People" intended — as is — in accordance with its original intent. In other words, it was interpreted exegetically (as textually constructed) rather than eisegetically (as a so-called "living constitution" that could be continually reinterpreted to express the biases of later generations of politicians and jurists).

But incrementally, constitutional Rule of Law in the United States has been diluted by the actions of those in the executive, legislative and judicial branches — most notably the latter — and at great hazard to the future of Liberty.

As Thomas Jefferson warned repeatedly, the greatest threat to Rule of Law and constitutional limitations on central government was an unbridled judiciary: "The original error [was in] establishing a judiciary independent of the nation, and which, from the citadel of the law, can turn its guns on those they were meant to defend, and control and fashion their proceedings to its own will. ... The opinion which gives to the judges the right to decide what laws are constitutional and what not, not only for themselves in their own sphere of action but for the Legislature and Executive also in their spheres, would make the Judiciary a despotic branch."

Jefferson clearly understood that, should our Constitution ever become a malleable document for a politicized and despotic judiciary to misinterpret according to executive and legislative special interests, Rule of Law would gradually yield to the rule of men — the historical terminus of the latter being tyranny.

Our Framers did not subject judges to election in order to avoid political corruption. They assumed judges would remain above such influences and stay true to Rule of Law, thus protecting our Constitution from avarice and populist adulteration. Our Founders and early members of the judiciary were certainly men of such character, and they were singularly devoted to Liberty and Rule of Law.

But as Jefferson predicted, many in the executive and legislative branches eventually abandoned their obligatory oaths "to Support and

Defend" our Constitution. Consequently, an ideologically appointed judiciary would suffer a similar fate of corruption, which would then be difficult to correct since judges are protected from electoral eviction. In effect, it may be argued that all three branches of government have devolved into "despotic" branches.

Regarding the process of amendment prescribed by our Constitution, George Washington wrote, "If in the opinion of the People the distribution or modification of the constitutional powers be in any particular wrong, let it be corrected by an amendment in the way which the Constitution designates, but let there be no change by usurpation; for though this in one instance may be the instrument of good, it is the customary weapon by which free governments are destroyed."

Alexander Hamilton concurred: "A sacred respect for the constitutional law is the vital principle, the sustaining energy of a free government." He also wrote, "The present Constitution is the standard to which we are to cling. Under its banners, bona fide must we combat our political foes — rejecting all changes but through the channel itself provides for amendments."

On the subject of constitutional interpretation, Jefferson wrote: "The Constitution on which our Union rests, shall be administered ... according to the safe and honest meaning contemplated by the plain understanding of the People of the United States at the time of its adoption — a meaning to be found in the explanations of those who advocated it. ... On every question of construction, carry ourselves back to the time when the Constitution was adopted, recollect the spirit manifested in the debates and instead of trying what meaning may be squeezed out of the text or invented against it, conform to the probable one in which it was passed."

Jefferson concluded, "Our peculiar security is in the possession of a written Constitution. Let us not make it a blank paper by construction."

James Madison agreed: "I entirely concur in the propriety of resorting to the sense in which the Constitution was accepted and ratified by the nation. In that sense alone it is the legitimate Constitution. And if that is not the guide in expounding it, there may be no security for a consistent and stable, more than for a faithful exercise of its powers."

Madison added, "As the Courts are generally the last in making the decision, it results to them by refusing or not refusing to execute a law to stamp it with its final character. This makes the Judiciary department paramount in fact to the Legislature, which was never intended, and can never be proper."

Justice James Wilson set forth, "The first and governing maxim in the interpretation of a statute is to discover the meaning of those who made it."

The Federalist Papers clearly delineate constitutional interpretation. In Federalist No. 78, Alexander Hamilton wrote, "[The judicial branch] may truly be said to have neither FORCE nor WILL, but merely judgment. ... Liberty can have nothing to fear from the judiciary alone, but would have everything to fear from its union with either of the other departments."

In Federalist No. 81, Hamilton declared, "There is not a syllable in the [Constitution] which directly empowers the national courts to construe the laws according to the spirit of the Constitution. ... The Constitution ought to be the standard of construction for the laws, and that wherever there is an evident opposition, the laws ought to give place to the Constitution." And yet this non-existent "spirit" is the essence of today's "living constitution" as amended by judicial diktat rather than its prescribed method in Article V.

The national courts have done great damage to our Constitution's original form and intent, errantly, regressively and perilously eroding Rule of Law and incrementally replacing it with the rule of men. The federal judiciary has indeed become the "despotic branch" that Jefferson warned of.

Shortly before his death, Jefferson wrote, "At the establishment of our constitutions, the judiciary bodies were supposed to be the most helpless and harmless members of the government. Experience, however, soon showed in what way they were to become the most dangerous; that the insufficiency of the means provided for their removal gave them a freehold and irresponsibility in office; that their decisions, seeming to concern individual suitors only, pass silent and unheeded by the public at large; that these decisions, nevertheless, become law by precedent, sapping, by little and little, the foundations of the constitution, and working its change by construction, before any one has perceived that that invisible and helpless worm has been busily employed in consuming its substance. In truth, man is not made to be trusted for life, if secured against all liability to account."

The Rule of Men

"The basis of our political systems is the right of the People to make and to alter their Constitutions of Government. But the Constitution which at any time exists, until changed by an explicit and authentic act of the whole People is sacredly obligatory upon all."
—George Washington

The first significant instance of constitutional interpretation by the federal judiciary was the 1803 case of *Marbury v. Madison*. The Supreme Court, under Chief Justice John Marshall, denied a plaintiff's claim because it relied on the Judiciary Act of 1789, which the court ruled unconstitutional.

Since that ruling, the Marbury precedent has been used by judicial activists to violate the limits of judicial power outlined in Article III of our Constitution. It has thus eroded Rule of Law and created a sort of quiet constitutional crisis that may ultimately be more ruinous to our nation than that which led to the War Between the States.

Prior to Woodrow Wilson's "progressive" presidency, and prior to Franklin Roosevelt's further expansion of the central government with his "New Deal" social welfare programs, the courts were still largely populated with originalists — that is, those who properly rendered legal interpretation based on the Constitution's "original intent." Because of this, Roosevelt was often at odds with the courts.

So determined was FDR to overstep the constitutional limits on the executive branch that in 1937 he attempted to increase the number of justices on the Supreme Court from nine to 15, with the expectation that his six newly minted appointees would give him a favorably predisposed activist majority. (It's no coincidence that the term "living constitution" was coined that same year.)

Roosevelt failed in his attempted coup, but during his unprecedented three terms in office (he died 11 weeks into his fourth term, and the 22nd Amendment, which set a two-term limit on the presidency, was passed by Congress in 1947 and ratified by the states in 1951), he appointed a whopping eight Supreme Court justices. Their activist rulings consistently allowed him to enact his New Deal policies and expand the power and scope of the state. A fair reading of history shows that his policies also helped prolong the Great Depression.

In effect, Roosevelt successfully converted the judicial branch from one of independent review according to Rule of Law into one of subservience according to the rule of men.

In its prescription for separating the judiciary from the executive branch, Federalist No. 73 notes, "Judges ... by being often associated with the Executive ... might be induced to embark too far in the political views of that magistrate, and thus a dangerous combination might by degrees be cemented between the executive and judiciary departments. It is impossible to keep the judges too distinct from every other avocation than that of expounding the laws. It is peculiarly dangerous to place them in a situation to be either corrupted or influenced by the Executive."

But by the mid-20th century, statist executives had all but co-opted the judiciary, and those who favor judicial despotism have been devitalizing Rule of Law ever since.

In the decades that followed, the notion of a "living constitution," one subject to contemporaneous judicial interpretation molded by political agendas, became the standard in federal courts. With increasing frequency, judicial activists — jurists who "legislate from the bench" by issuing rulings at the behest of like-minded special-interest constituencies — were nominated and confirmed to the Supreme Court.

This degradation in Rule of Law was codified by the Warren Court in *Trop v. Dulles* (1958). In that ruling, the High Court noted that the Constitution should comport with "evolving standards ... that mark the progress of a maturing society." In other words, the Warren Court concluded that the Constitution should be a fully pliable document, "a mere thing of wax in the hands of the judiciary which they may twist and shape into any form they please," as Thomas Jefferson had forewarned.

Since then, activist judges have not only undermined the plain language of our Constitution but have also done equal injury to the Bill of Rights.

By the 1980s, the adulteration of our Constitution by its Supreme Court arbiters was so commonplace that Justice Thurgood Marshall would frequently lecture on "The Constitution: A Living Document." He defended constitutional interpretation based upon contemporaneous moral, political and cultural circumstances.

More recently, the late Justice Antonin Scalia wrote, "[There's] the argument of flexibility and it goes something like this: The Constitution is over 200 years old and societies change. It has to change with society, like a living organism, or it will become brittle and break. But you would have to be an idiot to believe that; the Constitution is not a living organism; it is a legal document. It says something and doesn't say other things."

Justice Clarence Thomas followed, "There are really only two ways to interpret the Constitution — try to discern as best we can what the Framers intended or make it up. No matter how ingenious, imaginative or artfully put, unless interpretive methodologies are tied to the original intent of the Framers, they have no basis in the Constitution. ... To be sure, even the most conscientious effort to adhere to the original intent of the Framers of our Constitution is flawed, as all methodologies and human institutions are; but at least Originalism has the advantage of being legitimate and, I might add, impartial."

On the political consequences of a "living constitution," Justice Scalia concluded plainly, "If you think aficionados of a living constitution want to bring you flexibility, think again. ... As long as judges tinker with the Constitution to 'do what the people want,' instead of what the document actually commands, politicians who pick and confirm new federal judges will naturally want only those who agree with them politically."

Indeed, as Thomas Jefferson wrote, "In questions of power, then, let no more be heard of confidence in man, but bind him down from mischief by the chains of the Constitution."

A "Wall of Separation"?

"Congress shall make no law respecting an establishment of religion, or prohibiting the free exercise thereof; or abridging the freedom of speech, or of the press; or the right of the People peaceably to assemble, and to petition the Government for a redress of grievances."
—Article One, Bill of Rights

Among the most egregious examples of judicial activism undermining our Constitution are the many flawed rulings rendered in regard to Article One (the First Amendment) of the Bill of Rights, particularly to its assurance of religious freedom. Once again, in plain language, the First Amendment stipulates, "*Congress* shall make no law..."

But activist courts have ruled that this prohibition applies to virtually every public forum, from public schools and sporting events to public squares.

There is no more ominous assault on our Constitution, no more serious threat to Liberty "endowed," than that of the errant notion of utter separation between our constitutional government and our Creator. If knowledge of our Creator (at one time prevalent in every educational institution) is constrained, then the historically accepted knowledge that Liberty is "endowed by [our] Creator" will be equally diminished.

Our Founders' intent was that the central government would not favor one religious denomination over others by act of Congress. "Congress shall make no law..." It is precisely that which Thomas Jefferson referenced when noting the Constitution built "a wall of separation between church and State" — and nothing more.

But for decades, judicial activists have "interpreted" the First Amendment's "Establishment Clause" to suit their political agendas, placing severe constraints upon the free exercise of religion by invoking Jefferson's obscure and now wholly misrepresented "wall of separation" language

Advocates of the "living constitution" are intent upon removing faith from every public quarter, and they ironically and erroneously cite a once-obscure "wall of separation" metaphor from Thomas Jefferson's 1802 letter to the Danbury Baptists Association in Connecticut.

In 1802, Jefferson rightly supported the disestablishment of the Anglican Church as the official religion in Virginia. Baptists hoped he would similarly affirm the disestablishment of the Congregational Church in Connecticut, and moreover, that the national government would not declare Anglicanism the national church, much as the Crown recognized the Church of England as its official church. Such recognition led to discriminations against those who were not adherents of the official church.

Responding to the Baptists, Jefferson wrote, "I contemplate with solemn reverence that act of the whole American people which declared that their legislature should 'make no law respecting an establishment of religion, or prohibiting the free exercise thereof,' thus building a wall of separation between Church and State. ... I reciprocate your kind prayers for the protection and blessing of the common Father and Creator of man." (Notably, two days after writing that letter, Jefferson attended religious services in the House of Representatives.)

His letter, in fact, reaffirmed the Bill of Rights' barrier between federal and state governments, and the prohibition against Congress making any law "respecting an establishment of religion." His "separation" language most certainly *did not* create a prohibition against faith expression in any and all public venues, and yet that is how the courts interpret it today.

Again, the intended consequence of the contemporary artificial barrier between church and state is to remove references to our Creator from all public forums, particularly government education institutions, and thus, over time, to disabuse belief in a sovereign God and His endowment of Liberty — the innate rights of man.

Recall that this same Thomas Jefferson also proclaimed, "The God who gave us life, gave us Liberty at the same time. ... Can the liberties of a nation be thought secure when we have removed their only firm basis, a conviction in the minds of the People that these liberties are of the gift of God? That they are not to be violated but with his wrath? Indeed I tremble for my country when I reflect that God is just: that his justice cannot sleep for ever."

Indeed, "Life, Liberty and the pursuit of Happiness" are the Natural Rights of Man. They are *gifts from our God*, not government. And yet an activist judiciary would have us believe otherwise.

It was with firm regard for the Rights of Man that our Constitution was written and ratified "in order to secure the Blessings of Liberty to ourselves and our Posterity." As such, it established a constitutional republic whose foundation was laws based on Natural Rights, not rights allocated by governments or by those in positions of power.

"Our political way of life," John Quincy Adams wrote, "is by the Laws of Nature and of Nature's God, and of course presupposes the existence of God, the moral ruler of the universe, and a rule of right and wrong, of just and unjust, binding upon man, preceding all institutions of human society and government."

George Mason declared, "The laws of nature are the laws of God, whose authority can be superseded by no power on earth."

Notably, the conviction that our Rights are innately bestowed by "the Laws of Nature and of Nature's God" is enumerated in the constitutional preambles of every state in our Union.

"Let it simply be asked," George Washington wrote in his 1796 Farewell Address, "where is the security for property, for reputation, for life, if the sense of religious obligation deserts the oaths, which are the instruments of investigation in the Courts of Justice? And let us with caution indulge the supposition, that morality can be maintained without religion. Whatever may be conceded to the influence of refined education on minds of peculiar structure, reason and experience both forbid us to expect that National morality can prevail in exclusion of religious principle."

John Adams asserted, "Our constitution was made only for a moral and religious people. It is wholly inadequate to the government of any other."

As the late Chief Justice of the Supreme Court William Rehnquist protested, "The wall of separation between church and state is a metaphor based upon bad history, a metaphor which has proved useless as a guide to judging. It should be frankly and explicitly abandoned. ... The greatest injury of the 'wall' notion is its mischievous diversion of judges from the actual intention of the drafters of the Bill of Rights."

"The Palladium of the Liberties of the Republic"

"A well regulated Militia, being necessary to the security of a free State, the right of the People to keep and bear Arms, shall not be infringed." —Article Two, Bill of Rights

Article Two (the Second Amendment) was written as a proscription against government intrusion and usurpation upon all the other natural Rights of Man, because "the right of the People to keep and bear Arms" enables and empowers the defense of all other rights.

Indeed, this innate right can be viewed as the first civil right, since it is the fundamental guarantor of all other rights as affirmed by our Founders.

As previously noted, on April 19th, 1775, the first shots of the eight-year struggle for American independence were fired at Lexington and Concord, celebrated now as "Patriots' Day." "The Shot Heard Round the World" was in fact a response to the British government's attempt to seize weapons and disarm the people.

Three months later, on July 6th, 1775, the Continental Congress passed Thomas Jefferson's "Declaration of the Causes and Necessity for Taking Up Arms," asserting the right of the people to defend themselves against tyranny: "We most solemnly, before God and the world, declare, that, exerting the utmost energy of those powers, which our beneficent Creator hath graciously bestowed upon us, the arms we have been compelled by our enemies to assume, we will, in defiance of every hazard ... employ for the preservation of our liberties; being with one mind resolved to die freemen rather than to live slaves. ... With a humble confidence in the mercies of the Supreme and impartial God and Ruler of the Universe, we most devoutly implore His divine goodness to protect us happily through this great conflict."

During the 1788 Massachusetts Convention debates to ratify the U.S. Constitution, Samuel Adams stated, "The said Constitution shall never be construed ... to prevent the People of the United States who are peaceable citizens from keeping their own arms." Other states provided similar assurances in their constitutions, based on common law.

That same year, James Madison proposed what would become the Second Amendment in a speech advocating a Bill of Rights, a concession to the Anti-Federalists, who were concerned about essential Liberties under the Constitution. According to Madison, "The right of the people to keep and bear arms shall not be infringed; a well armed and well regulated militia being the best security of a free country..." (Notably, in Madison's construction of the Second Amendment, the right of the people to keep and bear arms is the primary clause — true as well in the text of the actual amendment, although the order of clauses has been reversed.)

Madison further defined the constitutional affirmation of this right in Federalist No. 46: "The ultimate authority ... resides in the People alone. ... The advantage of being armed, which the Americans possess over the people of almost every other nation ... forms a barrier against the enterprises of ambition, more insurmountable than any which a simple government of any form can admit of."

"What country can preserve its liberties," Jefferson asked rhetorically, "if their rulers are not warned from time to time that their people preserve the spirit of resistance? Let them take arms."

George Mason, author of the Virginia Bill of Rights (which was the inspiration for our Constitution's Bill of Rights), put it this way: "To disarm the people — that was the best and most effectual way to enslave them." He added, "I ask, sir, what is the militia? It is the whole people, except for a few public officials."

Indeed, the word "militia," in context, as repeatedly confirmed by the Supreme Court, refers to "the People" and their individual right to keep and bear arms.

George Washington's friend and Revolutionary War compatriot, Richard Henry Lee, wrote, "To preserve Liberty, it is essential that the whole body of the people always possess arms, and be taught alike, especially when young, how to use them."

Alexander Hamilton wrote, "If the representatives of the people betray their constituents, there is then no recourse left but in the exertion of that original right of self-defense which is paramount to all positive forms of government," adding, "Little more can reasonably be aimed at, with respect to the people at large, than to have them properly armed and equipped."

In his *Commentaries on the Constitution* (1833), Justice Joseph Story, appointed to the Supreme Court by James Madison, affirmed the pre-eminence of the Second Amendment: "The right of the citizens to keep and bear arms has justly been considered as the palladium of the liberties of a republic; since it offers a strong moral check against usurpation and arbitrary power of the rulers; and will generally, even if these are successful in the first instance, enable the People to resist and triumph over them."

Like Justice Story, Founder Noah Webster wrote, "Tyranny is the exercise of some power over a man, which is not warranted by law, or necessary for the public safety. A people can never be deprived of their liberties, while they retain in their own hands, a power sufficient to any other power in the state."

While the Second Amendment has not been specifically altered by another amendment since ratification, it most certainly has been subject to much alteration by judicial misinterpretation and overreach.

Statists in the executive and legislative branches, and their activists in the judicial branch, endeavor, wherever possible, to enfeeble and erode the Second Amendment, with the ultimate objective of disarming Americans and demoting their constitutional standing as citizens to their former standing as subjects.

"The Powers Not Delegated..."

"The powers not delegated to the United States by the Constitution, nor prohibited by it to the States, are reserved to the States respectively, or to the People." —Article Ten (the Tenth Amendment)

The federal government has, over the years, routinely violated this amendment by wielding all manner of legislative and regulatory powers — powers that should be, according to Rule of Law, "reserved to the States respectively, or to the People."

Equally injurious to our Constitution is the manner in which the assurance of states' rights outlined in the Tenth Amendment has been eroded by legislative malfeasance and judicial diktat.

In Federalist No. 39, James Madison expounded upon the covenantal nature of the states' would-be federal arrangement, voluntarily bound by mutual obligation. "Each State," he wrote, "in ratifying the Constitution, is considered as a sovereign body, independent of all others, and only to be bound by its own voluntary act. In this relation, then, the new Constitution will, if established, be a FEDERAL, and not a NATIONAL constitution."

In Federalist No. 45, Madison highlighted the definite limits placed upon power in such a federal structure, writing, "The powers delegated by the proposed Constitution to the federal government are few and defined. Those which are to remain in the State governments are numerous and indefinite."

To help ensure that the central government would not overstep its constitutional authority, Madison wrote in Federalist No. 46, "Ambitious encroachments of the federal government, on the authority of the State governments, would not excite the opposition of a single State, or of a few States only. They would be signals of general alarm. ... But what degree of madness could ever drive the federal government to such an extremity."

But by 1792, Madison foresaw the potential for abuse, and he protested loudly against the prospect of the new government's urge to redistribute the wealth of its citizens for purposes other than those expressly authorized by our Constitution: "If Congress can do whatever in their discretion can be done by money, and will promote the General Welfare, the Government is no longer a limited one, possessing enumerated powers, but an indefinite one, subject to particular exceptions."

Similarly, Jefferson wrote: "Giving [Congress] a distinct and independent power to do any act they please which may be good for the Union, would render all the preceding and subsequent enumerations of power completely useless. It would reduce the whole [Constitution] to a single phrase, that of instituting a Congress with power to do whatever would be for the good of the United States; and as sole judges of the good or evil, it would be also a power to do whatever evil they please. Certainly no such universal power was meant to be given them. [The Constitution] was intended to lace them up straightly within the enumerated powers and those without which, as means, these powers could not be carried into effect."

In his remarkable wisdom, Jefferson also warned that the legislature and courts should not enact laws so complex and convoluted as to conceal their meaning and implications from those for whom they were, ostensibly, created: "Laws are made for men of ordinary understanding and should, therefore, be construed by the ordinary rules of common sense. Their meaning is not to be sought for in metaphysical subtleties which may make anything mean everything or nothing at pleasure."

Unfortunately, the law today is barely comprehensible in its scope even to those who legislate and interpret it, and this has dire implications for the federalist system of government established by our Constitution.

"A Republic, if You Can Keep It"

"Our new Constitution is now established, and has an appearance that promises permanency; but in this world nothing can be said to be certain, except death and taxes." —Benjamin Franklin

As our Founders debated the language of our Constitution, Ben Franklin wrote, "I have so much faith in the general government of the world by Providence, that I can hardly conceive a transaction of such momentous importance to the welfare of millions now existing, and to exist in the posterity of a great nation, should be suffered to pass without being in some degree influenced, guided and governed by that omnipotent, omnipresent Beneficent Ruler, in whom all inferior spirits live & move and have their being."

At the close of the Constitutional Convention in Philadelphia, Franklin was asked by a citizen if the delegates had formed a republic or a monarchy. He responded famously, "A republic, if you can keep it."

To that end, as a warning for future generations to beware of "cunning, ambitious and unprincipled men," George Washington wrote, "A just estimate of that love of power, and proneness to abuse it, which predominates in the human heart is sufficient to satisfy us of the truth of this position."

"Good intentions," noted Daniel Webster, "will always be pleaded for every assumption of authority. It is hardly too strong to say that the Constitution was made to guard the People against the dangers of good intentions. There are men in all ages who mean to govern well, but they mean to govern. They promise to be good masters, but they mean to be masters."

Or, as Alexander Hamilton put it, "Of those men who have overturned the liberties of republics, the greatest number have begun their career by paying an obsequious court to the People, commencing demagogues and ending tyrants."

John Adams observed, "Is the present State of the Nation Republican enough? Is virtue the principle of our Government? Is honor? Or is ambition and avarice adulation, baseness, covetousness, the thirst of riches, indifference concerning the means of rising and enriching, the contempt of principle, the Spirit of party and of faction, the motive and the principle that governs?"

On the necessity of wisdom and reason, Thomas Jefferson wrote, "Man, once surrendering his reason, has no remaining guard against absurdities the most monstrous, and like a ship without rudder, is the sport of every wind. With such persons, gullibility takes the helm from the hand of reason and the mind becomes a wreck."

John Adams warned of dire consequences should such wisdom and reason fail to sustain Liberty as enshrined in our Constitution: "A

Constitution of Government once changed from Freedom, can never be restored. Liberty, once lost, is lost forever."

Unfortunately, and at the expense of our Liberty, the Constitution has suffered under generations of "cunning, ambitious and unprincipled" politicians and judges whose successors now recognize only vestiges of its original intent. Today, constitutional Rule of Law has been weakened by those who have failed to abide by their sacred oaths to "support and defend" the same.

As the erosion of constitutional authority undermines individual Liberty, it likewise undermines economic Liberty, and the primary instruments of that erosion are taxation and regulation.

Our Founders were uniformly concerned about government power to lay and collect taxes, most notably direct taxation of income, and, accordingly, enumerated specific limitations on taxing and spending.

James Madison addressed the issue of unlimited spending and warned that misconstruction of "the power 'to lay and collect taxes, duties, imposts, and excises, to pay the debts, and provide for the common defense and general welfare of the United States,' amounts to an unlimited commission to exercise every power which may be alleged to be necessary for the common defense or general welfare."

To ensure that federal taxation would be limited to these constraints, Article I, Section 8, Clause 1, of our Constitution (the "Taxing and Spending Clause"), as duly ratified in 1789, defined "Taxes, Duties, Imposts and Excises," but Section 8 required that such "shall be uniform throughout the United States." This, in effect, limited the power of Congress to impose direct taxes on individuals, as further outlined in Section 9: "No Capitation, or other direct, Tax shall be laid, unless in Proportion to the Census or enumeration herein before directed to be taken."

That constitutional limitation survived until 1861, when the first income tax was imposed to defray Union costs during the War Between the States. That three-percent tax on incomes over $800 was sold as an emergency war measure. In 1894, congressional Democrats tested the Constitution again, passing a peacetime tax of two percent on income above $4,000. A year later, that tariff was overturned by the Supreme Court as not complying with the limitations set forth in Article 1.

Perhaps the most devastating blow to economic Liberty, however, was dealt by the father of American socialism, Woodrow Wilson, who was elected in large part due to his mastery of classist rhetoric as outlined by Karl Marx's *Communist Manifesto* in the mid-19th century. Wilson used that rhetoric to gain rapid passage of the Sixteenth Amendment in 1913, which specified, "The Congress shall have power to lay and collect taxes on incomes, from whatever source derived, without apportionment among the several States, and without regard to any census or enumeration."

"From whatever source derived" indeed.

The top tax rate levied under the new amendment was seven percent on incomes above $500,000, but today, almost every individual with an income of $25,000 or more (less than $1,000 in 1914 dollars) is taxed. If Wilson had attempted to impose his tax on incomes of $1,000, a second American Revolution may well have commenced. But like most assaults on Liberty, the income tax levy has avoided insurrection by incremental imposition on ever-broader income groups over the past century.

James Madison's warning was prescient: "There are more instances of the abridgment of the freedom of the People by gradual and silent encroachments of those in power than by violent and sudden usurpations."

The Sixteenth Amendment has been used to enact unequal and discriminatory taxation of targeted groups of income classes — "progressive" taxation as it is known. The resulting classism is the bulwark of all socialist movements. The "class warfare" agenda opened the floodgates for populist executives and legislators to enact taxes for expenditures not expressly authorized by our Constitution, and thus, the end of constitutionally limited government and the empowerment of the rule of men.

Notably, however, the construction of the Sixteenth Amendment notwithstanding, Article I, Section 9, of our Constitution assures that "No Bill of Attainder or ex post facto Law shall be passed," as these would allow the targeting of individuals or minority groups for undue punishment. Thus, it should be argued that targeting certain classes of income earners constitutes a bill of attainder, which should disqualify all but the even distribution of taxation by way of a flat tax across the board.

The most reckless of the 20th century's class warfare provocateurs was Franklin D. Roosevelt, who was, ironically, an aristocrat. At the onset of the Great Depression, he instituted a plethora of policies that further challenged constitutional limits on our government, the cost of which now threatens our nation's economic solvency.

FDR's economic and social solutions were shaped by his upbringing as an "inheritance welfare liberal" (those raised dependent on inheritance rather than self-reliance). He used the Great Depression as cover to redefine and expand the role of the central government via countless extra-constitutional decrees, and he expanded Wilson's program for redistribution of wealth in order to fund those extra-constitutional efforts.

Roosevelt proclaimed, "Here is my principle: Taxes shall be levied according to ability to pay. That is the only American principle."

If that language sounds somehow familiar, it is because his unconstitutional "American principle" is essentially a paraphrase of Karl Marx's communist maxim, "From each according to his abilities, to each according to his needs."

Roosevelt's "principles" had no basis in Rule of Law or the principles of free enterprise. Consequently, his New Deal policies and programs set the standard for government expansion funded by wealth redistribution under what is the central government's most powerful weapon: The U.S. Tax Code.

As Chief Justice John Marshall wrote in *McCulloch v. Maryland* (1819): "An unlimited power to tax involves, necessarily, a power to destroy; because there is a limit beyond which no institution and no property can bear taxation."

But a century later under Wilson, government began to nibble around the edges. Today, it gobbles wholesale.

The net effect of this expansion was and remains an abject violation of our Constitution's Article Ten (the Tenth Amendment), which affirms: "The powers not delegated to the United States by the Constitution, nor prohibited by it to the States, are reserved to the States respectively, or to the people." The resulting corruption of constitutional Rule of Law has propagated a perilous assault on Liberty.

The Rise of Statism and the Welfare State

"I am for doing good to the poor, but I differ in opinion of the means. I think the best way of doing good to the poor, is not making them easy in poverty, but leading or driving them out of it. In my youth I travelled much, and I observed in different countries, that the more public provisions were made for the poor, the less they provided for themselves, and of course became poorer. And, on the contrary, the less was done for them, the more they did for themselves, and became richer." —Benjamin Franklin

The ability to impose direct taxes to support a welfare state was anathema to our Founders and the Liberty they fought to secure for their posterity.

Of government welfare programs, the Congressional Record notes that James Madison "acknowledged, for his own part, that he could not undertake to lay his finger on that article in the Federal Constitution which granted a right of Congress of expending, on objects of benevolence, the money of their constituents."

Neither Article 1, Section 8, of our Constitution, nor its Sixteenth Amendment, gave Congress the authority to collect taxes for bailing out financial institutions, or subsidizing industries such as manufacturing and health care, or funding education and welfare, or issuing tens of thousands of earmarks for special interest "pork" projects. Nor is Congress authorized to institute countless conditions for the redistribution of wealth in its more than 75,000 pages and four million words of tax code alone, or to impose millions of regulations on everything from carbon emissions to toilet water volume.

So corrupt is this process of funding special interests in return for campaign contributions that it is now a grave threat to our Constitution.

Put another way, a large percentage of income is confiscated by the government and redistributed for purposes not expressly authorized by our Constitution. Consequently, our federal government has in recent years saddled the nation with more debt than in all its past history combined — debt that obligates future generations for repayment.

Of such debt, Jefferson concluded, "The principle of spending money to be paid by posterity, under the name of funding, is but swindling futurity on a large scale." This debt burden will, unless it is reversed, break the back of our nation's free enterprise system and permanently replace it with the statist policies of Democratic Socialism.

Washington warned, "Avoid likewise the accumulation of debt ... not ungenerously throwing upon posterity the burden which we ourselves ought to bear."

However, historians and economists concur that Democratic Socialism, like National Socialism, is tantamount to Marxist Socialism repackaged. It seeks a centrally planned economy directed by a single-party state that controls economic production via regulation and income redistribution. All three socialist manifestations are formed around class-warfare propaganda and are in direct opposition to free enterprise. As noted economist and philosopher F.A. Hayek wrote, "There is no difference in principle, between the economic philosophy of Nazism, socialism, communism, and fascism and that of the American welfare state and regulated economy."

Our Founders' wisdom notwithstanding, today, more than 70 percent of the federal budget is allocated for "objects of benevolence" for which there is no original constitutional authority. Despite claims to the contrary, the debt issue is not a government revenue problem but, rather, a government spending problem.

At this writing, taxes on the top 50 percent of income earners total almost 97 percent of government revenue, while some 40 percent of Americans bore virtually no direct cost of government. Much more ominous is the fact that almost 35 percent of Americans are now dependent upon redistributed wealth. Thus, they are predisposed to vote for those promising such redistribution rather than working for their own prosperity. Indeed, in the words of socialist playwright George Bernard Shaw, "A government which robs Peter to pay Paul can always depend on the support of Paul."

Under siege of oppressive taxation, regulation and debt accumulation, can our republic survive? Can Liberty long endure?

Principium Imprimis — Restoring First Principles

"In disquisitions of every kind there are certain primary truths, or first principles, upon which all subsequent reasoning must depend."
—*Alexander Hamilton*

If we are to bequeath to our posterity the Liberty that our Founders enshrined, then we must return to *principium imprimis*, or First Principles. Our freedoms cannot long endure unless we, the People, reaffirm what was well understood by our Founders: Liberty is "endowed by [our] Creator." The primacy of faith must be protected in order to preserve the most fundamental conviction that, as Jefferson wrote, our "liberties are the gift of God" and not the gift of government.

We must be steadfast in our advocacy for individual rights and responsibilities, and we must demand restoration of constitutional limits on government and the judiciary. We must be tireless in our promotion of traditional American values, particularly those family values that are the cornerstone of democratic society. We must support free enterprise in order that all Americans have the opportunity for prosperity, and a strong national defense to protect our national interests.

The Cycle of Democracy has been summarized as follows: from bondage (rule of men) to spiritual faith; from spiritual faith to great courage; from courage to Liberty (Rule of Law); from Liberty to abundance; from abundance to complacency; from complacency to apathy; from apathy to dependence; from dependence back into bondage (rule of men).

Our Founders established a democratic republic, not a democracy, in order to enfeeble this cycle. However, with the erosion of constitutional authority, our republic is now in jeopardy of following in the footsteps of all other republics throughout history. Only intervention by citizens and leaders who fight for the primacy of constitutional Rule of Law, those committed to supporting and defending the foundation of Liberty above their self-interest, will secure the republic for future generations.

Our Founders understood that such self-interest would undermine Liberty.

John Hancock wrote, "Suffer not yourselves to be betrayed, by the soft arts of luxury and effeminacy, into the pit digged for your destruction. ... I thank God that America abounds in men who are superior to all temptation, whom nothing can divert from a steady pursuit of the interest of their country, who are at once its ornament and safeguard."

Irrevocably linked to the rights ensured by constitutional Rule of Law is economic Liberty.

In 1916, an outspoken advocate for Liberty, a Presbyterian minister named William J. H. Boetcker, published a tract entitled "The Ten Cannots." It fittingly contrasts the competing political and economic agendas of the Right and Left in our modern era:

"You cannot bring about prosperity by discouraging thrift.

"You cannot strengthen the weak by weakening the strong.

"You cannot help the poor man by destroying the rich.

"You cannot further the brotherhood of man by inciting class hatred.

"You cannot build character and courage by taking away man's initiative and independence.

"You cannot help small men by tearing down big men.

"You cannot lift the wage earner by pulling down the wage payer.

"You cannot keep out of trouble by spending more than your income.

"You cannot establish security on borrowed money.

"You cannot help men permanently by doing for them what they will not do for themselves."

Simply put, the central government cannot give to anybody what it does not first take from somebody else.

Nineteenth century historian Alexis de Tocqueville once observed, "Democracy and socialism have nothing in common but one word: equality. But notice the difference: while democracy seeks equality in Liberty, socialism seeks equality in restraint and servitude."

Tocqueville was commenting on Liberty and free enterprise, American style, versus socialism as envisioned by emerging protagonists of centralized state governments. And he saw on the horizon a looming threat — a threat that would challenge freedoms writ in the blood and toil of our nation's Founders and generations since.

So what's a Patriot to do?

Extending Our Legacy of Liberty to the Next Generation

"Contemplate the mangled bodies of your countrymen, and then say 'what should be the reward of such sacrifices?'... If ye love wealth better than Liberty, the tranquility of servitude than the animated contest of freedom, go from us in peace. We ask not your counsels or arms. Crouch down and lick the hands which feed you. May your chains sit lightly upon you, and may posterity forget that you were our countrymen!" —Samuel Adams

Some of our countrymen are overwhelmed with the current state of our nation. They have resorted to fratricide within their ranks, or withdrawn from the fields of battle altogether. In so doing, they have forsaken the legacy of Liberty extended to them by generations of Patriots who have sacrificed their lives, their fortunes and their sacred honor.

Of such resignation, Jefferson declared, "Honor, justice, and humanity, forbid us tamely to surrender that freedom which we received from our gallant ancestors, and which our innocent posterity have a right to receive from us. We cannot endure the infamy and guilt of resigning succeeding generations to that wretchedness which inevitably awaits them if we basely entail hereditary bondage on them."

On retreating from the defense of Liberty, Benjamin Franklin wrote, "Those who would give up essential Liberty, to purchase a little temporary Safety, deserve neither Liberty nor Safety."

George Washington warned, "Disorders and miseries ... gradually incline the minds of men to seek security and repose in the absolute power of an Individual ... [who] turns this disposition to the purposes of his own elevation, on the ruins of Public Liberty. ... The spirit of encroachment tends to consolidate the powers of all the departments in one, and thus to create, whatever the form of government, a real despotism. ... Let there be no change by usurpation; for though this, in one instance, may be the instrument of good, it is the customary weapon by which free governments are destroyed."

"Is life so dear or peace so sweet," asked Patrick Henry, "as to be purchased at the price of chains and slavery? Forbid it, Almighty God! I know not what course others may take, but as for me, give me Liberty or give me death!"

In the same vein, Alexander Hamilton wrote, "A nation which can prefer disgrace to danger is prepared for a master, and deserves one!"

On Patriotism, George Washington, in his Farewell Address, said, "Citizens by birth or choice of a common country, that country has a right to concentrate your affections. The name of American, which belongs to you, in your national capacity, must always exalt the just pride of Patriotism, more than any appellation derived from local discriminations. ... Of all the dispositions and habits, which lead to political prosperity, Religion and morality are indispensible supports. In vain would that man claim the tribute of patriotism who should labor to subvert these great Pillars of human happiness — these firmest props of the duties of men and citizens."

But Washington also warned, "Guard against the impostures of pretended patriotism."

Plainly, none can claim the name "American Patriot" while passively submitting to laws and regulations that violate the most fundamental tenets of our Constitution.

At its core, the word "Patriot" has direct lineage to those who fought for American independence and established our constitutional republic. That lineage has descended through our history most conspicuously by way of those who have pledged "to Support and Defend" our Constitution — those who have been faithful to and have abided by their oaths, even unto death.

Those who can rightly claim the name Patriot in this era — men and women who have stood firm in defense of Liberty — are rightly encouraged by the grassroots groundswell of activism across the nation in recent years. Increasing numbers of our countrymen are awakening to the serious threats to our Constitution and their irrevocable terminus: tyranny.

The growing chorus of Patriot voices from every corner of the nation and all walks of life is demanding restoration of Rule of Law as enshrined in our Constitution.

Today's Patriots exemplify not only the eternal spirit of Liberty conferred by previous generations of Patriots, but also a spirit enlivened in recent history by a constitutional advocate who many historians regard as the greatest American president of the 20th century.

A Time for Choosing

"It is [the citizens] choice, and depends upon their conduct, whether they will be respectable and prosperous, or contemptable and miserable as a Nation. This is the time of their political probation; this is the moment when the eyes of the World are turned upon them."
                    —*George Washington*

Ronald Reagan was elected president in 1980 on a platform of constitutional integrity and federalism, and he was devoted to that doctrine. Four years later he was re-elected on those same principles in a landslide, winning every state but his opponent's home state (and, tellingly, the District of Columbia). Under his leadership, the nation's slide into the socialist abyss was arrested.

In 1964, years before he expressed any presidential aspirations, Reagan delivered a treatise on Liberty titled, "A Time for Choosing," which to this day appositely frames conservative philosophy.

In "The Speech," as we now know it, Reagan insisted that, "I think it's time we ask ourselves if we still know the freedoms that were intended for us by the Founding Fathers. ... Whether we believe in our capacity for self-government or whether we abandon the American Revolution and confess that a little intellectual elite in a far-distant capital can plan our lives for us better than we can plan them ourselves."

He continued: "You and I are told increasingly that we have to choose between a left or right, but I would like to suggest that there is no such thing as a left or right. There is only an up or down — up to a man's age-old dream; the ultimate in individual freedom consistent with law and order — or down to the ant heap of totalitarianism, and regardless of their sincerity, their humanitarian motives, those who would trade our freedom for security have embarked on this downward course."

Reagan departed the Democrat Party at the dawn of his political career, but he made a point to clarify his decision: "I didn't leave the Democratic Party; the Democratic Party left me."

Consistent with that assertion, contemporary leaders of the once-noble "party of the People" have turned the wisdom of their iconic sovereigns upside down.

In his 1961 Inaugural Address, President John F. Kennedy proclaimed, "My fellow Americans: Ask not what your country can do for you, ask what you can do for your country."

But today, his party insists: "Ask not what you can do for your country, ask what your country can do for you."

In his famous 1963 address from the Lincoln Memorial, Martin Luther King Jr. proclaimed, "I have a dream that my children will one day live in a nation where they will not be judged by the color of their skin but by the content of their character."

But now, his party asserts: "I have a dream that my children will be judged by the color of their skin, not the content of their character."

Some said President Reagan won broad support because he was a "great communicator," but he corrected that in his Farewell Address: "I wasn't a great communicator, but I communicated great things, and they didn't spring full bloom from my brow, they came from the heart of a great nation — from our experience, our wisdom, and our belief in principles that have guided us for two centuries."

The principles of Liberty advanced by President Reagan were, and remain, a template for the victory of Liberty over tyranny.

But our Legacy of Liberty is at risk today because so many Americans are utterly unable to articulate the difference between Rule of Law and rule of men. The consequence of such perilous ignorance is the rise of a regressive ideology whose agenda is, according to the Democrat Party's 2009-2017 standard-bearer, "fundamentally transforming the United States of America" through the transformation of our economic, social and cultural principles.

Thomas Jefferson warned in successive letters, "I place economy among the first and most important virtues and public debt as the greatest dangers to be feared. ... To preserve independence ... we must not let our rulers load us with perpetual debt. ... When all government ... shall be drawn to Washington as the center of all power, it will render powerless the checks provided of one government on another. ... Were we directed from Washington when to sow, and when to reap, we should soon want bread. ... The fore horse of this frightful team is public debt. Taxation follow that, and in its turn wretchedness and oppression."

Today, our economy is struggling under the enormous weight of mounting debt, and it may yet implode with much greater consequences than those of the Great Depression. The ensuing social crisis would result in government intervention under the pretense of "economic recovery," structured to, ultimately, replace the last vestiges of free enterprise with a Democratic Socialist framework.

As Jefferson concluded, "We must make our election between economy and Liberty, or profusion and servitude."

Alexander Hamilton wrote likewise, "No man in his senses can hesitate in choosing to be free, rather than a slave."

Another Time for Choosing

"If men of wisdom and knowledge, of moderation and temperance, of patience, fortitude and perseverance, of sobriety and true republican simplicity of manners, of zeal for the honour of the Supreme Being and the welfare of the commonwealth; if men possessed of these other excellent qualities are chosen to fill the seats of government, we may expect that our affairs will rest on a solid and permanent foundation." —Samuel Adams

Given that so many actions and regulations handed down by those in the executive, legislative and judicial branches fail to comport with the plain language and authority of our Constitution, it is clear that they have abandoned their "sacred oaths" to "support and defend" that venerable document "against all enemies, foreign and domestic," and to "bear true faith and allegiance to the same."

Our Founders understood that Rule of Law as enshrined in our Constitution was the foundational guarantee to protect and sustain Liberty for their generation and that of their posterity. Consequently, they prescribed that all elected officials be bound by sacred oath to "support and defend" our Constitution.

For presidents, Article II, Section 1, of our Constitution specifies: "Before he enter on the Execution of his Office, he shall take the following Oath or Affirmation: 'I do solemnly swear (or affirm) that I will faithfully execute the Office of President of the United States, and will to the best of my Ability, preserve, protect and defend the Constitution of the United States.'"

Likewise Article VI, Clause 3, specifies: "The Senators and Representatives before mentioned, and the Members of the several

State Legislatures, and all executive and judicial Officers, both of the United States and of the several States, shall be bound by Oath or Affirmation, to support this Constitution."

In the current era, however, many federal officeholders have forsaken their oaths and instead focus on redistributing wealth to their special-interest constituencies in order to perpetuate their own re-election. Here, we can be certain that when the number of constituents who vote for their income and provisions outnumber those who work for their income and provisions, the republic will be lost.

The time has come to inquire with a unified voice: If there is no explicit constitutional authority for the laws and regulations enacted by Congress and enforced by the central government, then by what authority do those entities lay and collect taxes to fund such laws and regulations? If they have no authority, does this then constitute "taxation without representation"? What should be the punishment for their dereliction?

Today, while the words "conservative" and "liberal" are ubiquitously used to describe political alliances, these words more essentially describe whether one advocates for Rule of Law or for the rule of men; the conservation of our Constitution as the Founders intended, or its leftist interpretation by regressive legislators and judicial activists.

As Reagan challenged, it is time for each of us to choose which of these we advocate and to fully understand the consequences of that choice. It is time for those of us who endorse the most basic tenets of our republic — "That all men are created equal," that they are in fact "endowed by their Creator with certain unalienable Rights," and "that among these are Life, Liberty and the pursuit of Happiness" — to honor that heritage and set about the formidable task of restoring individual Liberty and constitutional limits upon the branches of our federal government.

The futility of debating policy matters must now yield to a more substantive national debate about constitutional authority and the First Principles of Liberty.

If we are to fully restore Liberty and the integrity of our Constitution, we must continue to do so from the bottom up, a groundswell from the grassroots. Indeed, nothing great and enduring has ever been built from the top down. We must therefore start at the foundation, speaking with one disciplined, determined and unified voice toward one primary objective: the re-establishment of Rule of Law.

If we are to succeed, we must understand our Constitution and the Rule of Law it enshrines, and we must extend that understanding to others. If we are to turn back the rising tide of tyranny, it is important that every American Patriot, all of whom are committed to preserving our constitutional heritage and extending our legacy of Liberty to future generations, be able to articulate the difference between Rule of Law and rule of men.

Indeed, in this, the third century since our foundational Declaration and Constitution were instituted, quiet encroachments have resulted in a central government poised to dictate the terms of Liberty according to the decrees of men. The threat of tyranny is imminent.

Although our Constitution provides the people with an authentic means for amendment, as prescribed in Article V, activist jurists and lawmakers have altered that founding convention well beyond any semblance of its original intent, using the courts, legislation and regulation to greatly expand the powers of the central government according to their decrees.

We must declare by all means that the scope of our government's activities be constrained to the limits enumerated in our Constitution, and we must understand that this contraction will require courage, deliberation and years of steadfast diligence. It will take time to rebuild from generations of erosion to Rule of Law. But rebuild we must, and with determination. For if we fail, and Rule of Law is overwhelmed by the rule of men, tyranny will, once again, prevail.

On July 4th, 1776, our Declaration of Independence was inaugurated as our nation's supreme contract, proclaiming the unalienable Rights of Man. It asserted, "That whenever any Form of Government becomes destructive of these ends, it is the Right of the People to alter or to abolish it, and to institute new Government." Our Declaration's principal author, Thomas Jefferson, wrote, "The tree of Liberty must be refreshed from time to time with the blood of patriots and tyrants. ... Resistance to tyrants is obedience to God." On the signing of the Declaration, John Adams noted, "I am well aware of the toil and blood and treasure that it will cost to maintain this Declaration."

While one prays that Liberty will be restored and extended to our posterity by way of spirited electoral rebellion — ballots rather than bullets — history does not favor such prospects. But the beauty of our constitutional republic, as reinforced in recent years, is that an informed electorate can reverse by way of the ballot box the trends toward tyranny.

Founder Patrick Henry wrote of seemingly benign encroachments upon Liberty, "It is natural to man to indulge in the illusions of hope. We are apt to shut our eyes against a painful truth — and listen to the song of that syren... For my part, whatever anguish of spirit it might cost, I am willing to know the whole truth; to know the worst, and to provide for it."

It is time to fully object to the degraded state of our Constitution and reject any further degradation by way of "illusions of hope" that these depredations will magically repair themselves. It is the responsibility of our generation of Patriots to provide for its revitalization. In the spirit of Thomas Paine's 1776 assertion, "If there must be trouble, let it be in my day, that my child may have peace," so too it should be in our day.

As the means for restoring the integrity of our Constitution are weighed, in regard to a "constitutional convention" for amendment, let us beware. In this day of mass communication and mass manipulation, there may be severe unintended consequences to such a convention.

Here, let us consider an alternative, a "Constitutional Confederation of States," an alliance of states whose delegations would assemble to re-affirm the authority of our Constitution — in effect, to re-ratify it and the Rule of Law it enshrines.

Article IV, Section 4, prescribes with no ambiguity, "The United States shall guarantee to every state in this union a republican form of government..." A Constitutional Confederation of States should demand no less than the federalism prescribed by our Constitution and affirmed in its Tenth Amendment.

Ronald Reagan said, "There are no easy answers, but there are simple answers. We must have the courage to do what we know is morally right. ... You and I have a rendezvous with destiny. We will preserve for our children this, the last best hope of man on earth, or we will sentence them to take the last step into a thousand years of darkness."

Liberty or Tyranny?

"The citizens of the United States are responsible for the greatest trust ever confided to a political society. If justice, good faith, honor, gratitude and all the other qualities which ennoble the character of a nation and fulfill the ends of government be the fruits of our establishments, the cause of Liberty will acquire a dignity and lustre, which it has never yet enjoyed, and an example will be set, which cannot but have the most favourable influence on the Rights on Mankind. If on the other side, our governments should be unfortunately blotted with the reverse of these cardinal and essential virtues, the great cause which we have engaged to vindicate, will be dishonored and betrayed; the last and fairest experiment in favor of the Rights of human nature will be turned against them; and their patrons and friends exposed to be insulted and silenced by the votaries of tyranny and usurpation." —James Madison

The cause of, and necessity for, the American Revolution was the violation of fundamental rights endowed by the Laws of Nature and Nature's God. Unjust taxation was the catalyst for the first American

Revolution and the attempt to disarm the People resulted in the "Shot Heard Round the World."

Once again, the irrevocable "Rights of Man" are being violated, and that encroachment is sustained by wealth confiscation and redistribution, and by regulation, for purposes not expressly authorized by our Constitution. As was the case at the dawn of the American Revolution, taxes and regulations are the catalysts for undermining our rights. Liberty is not secure for us, nor for our posterity, if the legislature institutes regulations, collects taxes and accumulates insurmountable obligations of debt to support government agendas and expenditures that are clearly outside the limits of our Constitution.

Consequently, our nation approaches the precipice of insolvency, and the bill is rapidly coming due. It will most certainly be repaid in the currency of tyranny unless Liberty and Rule of Law prevail.

Our Constitution, as written and ratified, stipulates in its preface that it is "ordained and established" by the People to "secure the Blessings of Liberty to ourselves and our Posterity." But the incremental revocation of our ability to defend ourselves from encroachments on our rights has greatly diminished our capacity to secure those blessing today, let alone for future generations.

"We, the People of the United States," must demand that members of the executive, legislative and judicial branches of the federal government abide by their sworn oaths to "support and defend" our Constitution as mandated in Article II and Article VI. The enforcement of regulations, the collection of taxes and the accumulation of debt for expenditures that have no express constitutional authorization is in violation of our Constitution and, thus, the oaths of those sworn to uphold it as the supreme law of the land.

"Representation" does not exist where there is no assurance that elected representatives will abide by their oaths to obey Rule of Law. As George Washington observed, "Where is the security for property, for reputation, for life, if the sense of religious obligation deserts the oaths?" Those representatives who undertake unlawful expenditures of the treasury as an instrument to perpetuate their re-election, whose allegiance is secured with confiscated and redistributed wealth, betray their oaths and do damage to our Constitution and our Liberty.

We as American Patriots must, "with a firm reliance on the protection of divine Providence, mutually pledge to each other our Lives, our Fortunes and our sacred Honor," as we endeavor to restore Rule of Law and our Constitution's limits on governmental power. As 18th century Irish statesman Edmund Burke, who supported the American Revolution, said of complacency and indifference, "When bad men combine, the good must associate; else they will fall one by one, an unpitied sacrifice in a contemptible struggle."

Likewise, on this critical need for association, on July 4th, 1776, Ben Franklin advised, "We must all hang together, or assuredly we shall all hang separately." This is sage advice for today and for all those days to come.

Fellow Patriots, at the dawn of the first fight for American Liberty, Thomas Paine wrote, "These are the times that try men's souls." And so it is today.

This treatise on Liberty is not a call for revolution but for restoration — to undertake whatever measures are dictated by prudence and necessity to restore the integrity and primacy of our Constitution and the Liberty it enshrines.

Take heart in these timeless words of George Washington, who penned them when it seemed that the first American Revolution might fail: "We should never despair. Our situation before has been unpromising and has changed for the better, so I trust, it will again. If new difficulties arise, we must only put forth new exertions and proportion our efforts to the exigency of the times."

Remember the words of Samuel Adams: "Let us consider, brethren, we are struggling for our best birthrights and inheritance... Let us disappoint the Men who are raising themselves on the ruin of this Country."

Fellow Patriots, only time separates our obligations from those of past Patriots, who were much as we are today. For, in Washington's words, "Our cause is noble; it is the cause of mankind!"

First and foremost, we are defenders of Liberty and First Principles. We are not defined by race, creed, ethnicity, religion, wealth, education, geography or political affiliation. Rather, we are defined by our devotion to the endowments of our Creator, and to the Liberty He has entrusted to us, one and all.

We are mothers, fathers and other family members nurturing the next generation of Patriots. We are farmers, craftsmen, tradesmen and industrial producers. We are small-business owners, service providers and professionals in medicine and law. We are employees and employers. We are in ministry at home and missionaries abroad. We are students and professors at colleges and universities, often standing alone for what is good and right.

We are Soldiers, Sailors, Airmen, Marines, Coast Guardsmen and public servants standing in harm's way at home and around the world, who are loyal, first and foremost, to a solemn oath to "support and defend" our Constitution.

We are consumers and taxpayers. And we are voters.

We are Patriot sons and daughters from all walks of life, heirs to the blessings of Liberty bequeathed to us at great personal cost by our Patriot forebears, confirmed in the opinion that it is our duty to God and country to extend those blessings to our posterity, and avowed upon our sacred honor to that end. We are vigilant, strong, prepared and faithful.

Make it known far and wide that we remain steadfast in our duty to extend the legacy of Liberty to the next generation, and upon our sacred honor we affirm that obligation. We will make no peace with any measure of oppression.

In 1630, Pilgrim John Winthrop, the first governor of Massachusetts, wrote, "For we must consider that we shall be as a City upon a hill. The eyes of all people are upon us."

On the eve of his first election in 1980, Ronald Reagan declared: "Let us resolve tonight that young Americans will always see those Potomac lights; that they will always find there a city of hope in a country that is free. And let us resolve they will say of our day and our generation that we did keep faith with our God, that we did act 'worthy of ourselves'; that we did protect and pass on lovingly that shining city on a hill."

He concluded his last national address in 1992, saying: "My fondest hope for each one of you — and especially for the young people here — is that you will love your country, not for her power or wealth, but for her selflessness and her idealism. May each of you have the heart to conceive, the understanding to direct, and the hand to execute works that will make the world a little better for your having been here. May all of you as Americans never forget your heroic origins, never fail to seek divine guidance, and never lose your natural, God-given optimism. And finally, my fellow Americans, may every dawn be a great new beginning for America and every evening bring us closer to that shining city upon a hill."

Finally, hold fast to these words of encouragement from President Reagan: "America's best days are yet to come. Our proudest moments are yet to be. Our most glorious achievements are just ahead."

For indeed they are!

Semper Vigilans Fortis Paratus et Fidelis
Pro Deo et Libertate — 1776

Mark Alexander
Publisher of *The Patriot Post*

ESSENTIAL QUESTIONS

1. Why did the Sons of Liberty throw chests of tea into Boston Harbor?

2. What was the purpose of the First and Second Continental Congress Conventions?

3. Our Declaration of Independence was derived from common law, "the Laws of Nature and Nature's God," all men being "endowed by their Creator with certain unalienable Rights." What is the importance of the assertion that these rights are "endowed by [our] Creator"?

4. What is Rule of Law, and what is its source?

5. What is rule of man and how does it differ from Rule of Law?

6. As publicly declared in the Declaration of Independence, what were our Founding Fathers willing to sacrifice?

7. What was the purpose of the Philadelphia Convention in 1787?

8. What are *The Federalist Papers*?

9. Who were the anti-Federalists, and why did they oppose the Constitution?

10. When were the Constitution and the Bill of Rights ratified?

11. Why did some Founders object to a Bill of Rights?

12. Did the Constitution establish the United States as a democracy?

13. What is a "living constitution," and what are its implications?

14. What was Thomas Jefferson's concern about judicial power?

15. Did the Founders create a "Wall of Separation" between church and state?

16. Who does the First Amendment prohibit from making any law respecting an establishment of religion, or prohibiting the free exercise thereof?

17. What is the importance of the Second Amendment?

18. What did Justice Joseph Story say about the Second Amendment?

19. What does the Tenth Amendment specify in terms of powers reserved by the states and the people?

20. What is the most oppressive means the central government has at its disposal to regulate the economy?

21. What did James Madison say about welfare and government spending on the objects of benevolence?

22. Does the government have the authority to collect taxes for payment of expenditures not authorized by our Constitution?

23. What did Justice John Marshall say about the power to tax?

24. What are the key elements of the oaths taken by all national officers and military personnel, and what is their obligation?

25. When debating any political or policy issue, why is it important to begin that debate with First Principles — what our Constitution actually authorizes government to do?

THE DECLARATION OF INDEPENDENCE

IN CONGRESS, JULY 4, 1776

The unanimous Declaration
of the thirteen united States of America,

When in the Course of human events, it becomes necessary for one people to dissolve the political bands which have connected them with another, and to assume among the powers of the earth, the separate and equal station to which the Laws of Nature and of Nature's God entitle them, a decent respect to the opinions of mankind requires that they should declare the causes which impel them to the separation.

We hold these truths to be self-evident, that all men are created equal, that they are endowed by their Creator with certain unalienable Rights, that among these are Life, Liberty and the pursuit of Happiness.–That to secure these rights, Governments are instituted among Men, deriving their just powers from the consent of the governed, –That whenever any Form of Government becomes destructive of these ends, it is the Right of the People to alter or to abolish it, and to institute new Government, laying its foundation on such principles and organizing its powers in such form, as to them shall seem most likely to effect their Safety and Happiness. Prudence, indeed, will dictate that Governments long established should not be changed for light and transient causes; and accordingly all experience hath shewn, that mankind are more disposed to suffer, while evils are sufferable, than to right themselves by abolishing the forms to which they are accustomed. But when a long train of abuses and usurpations, pursuing invariably the same Object evinces a design to reduce them under absolute Despotism, it is their right, it is their duty, to throw off such Government, and to provide new Guards for their future security.–Such has been the patient sufferance of these Colonies; and such is now the necessity which constrains them to alter their former Systems of Government. The history of the present King of Great Britain is a history of repeated injuries and usurpations, all having in direct object the establishment of an absolute Tyranny over these States. To prove this, let Facts be submitted to a candid world.

He has refused his Assent to Laws, the most wholesome and necessary for the public good.

He has forbidden his Governors to pass Laws of immediate and pressing importance, unless suspended in their operation till his Assent should be obtained; and when so suspended, he has utterly neglected to attend to them.

He has refused to pass other Laws for the accommodation of large districts of people, unless those people would relinquish the right of Representation in the Legislature, a right inestimable to them and formidable to tyrants only.

He has called together legislative bodies at places unusual, uncomfortable, and distant from the depository of their public Records, for the sole purpose of fatiguing them into compliance with his measures.

He has dissolved Representative Houses repeatedly, for opposing with manly firmness his invasions on the rights of the people.

He has refused for a long time, after such dissolutions, to cause others to be elected; whereby the Legislative powers, incapable of Annihilation, have returned to the People at large for their exercise; the State remaining in the mean time exposed to all the dangers of invasion from without, and convulsions within.

He has endeavoured to prevent the population of these States; for that purpose obstructing the Laws for Naturalization of Foreigners; refusing to pass others to encourage their migrations hither, and raising the conditions of new Appropriations of Lands.

He has obstructed the Administration of Justice, by refusing his Assent to Laws for establishing Judiciary powers.

He has made Judges dependent on his Will alone, for the tenure of their offices, and the amount and payment of their salaries.

He has erected a multitude of New Offices, and sent hither swarms of Officers to harrass our people, and eat out their substance.

He has kept among us, in times of peace, Standing Armies without the Consent of our legislatures.

He has affected to render the Military independent of and superior to the Civil power.

He has combined with others to subject us to a jurisdiction foreign to our constitution, and unacknowledged by our laws; giving his Assent to their Acts of pretended Legislation:

For Quartering large bodies of armed troops among us:

For protecting them, by a mock Trial, from punishment for any Murders which they should commit on the Inhabitants of these States:

For cutting off our Trade with all parts of the world:

For imposing Taxes on us without our Consent:

For depriving us in many cases, of the benefits of Trial by Jury:

For transporting us beyond Seas to be tried for pretended offences:

For abolishing the free System of English Laws in a neighbouring Province, establishing therein an Arbitrary government, and enlarging its Boundaries so as to render it at once an example and fit instrument for introducing the same absolute rule into these Colonies:

For taking away our Charters, abolishing our most valuable Laws, and altering fundamentally the Forms of our Governments:

For suspending our own Legislatures, and declaring themselves invested with power to legislate for us in all cases whatsoever.

He has abdicated Government here, by declaring us out of his Protection and waging War against us.

He has plundered our seas, ravaged our Coasts, burnt our towns, and destroyed the lives of our people.

He is at this time transporting large Armies of foreign Mercenaries to compleat the works of death, desolation and tyranny, already begun with circumstances of Cruelty & perfidy scarcely paralleled in the most barbarous ages, and totally unworthy the Head of a civilized nation.

He has constrained our fellow Citizens taken Captive on the high Seas to bear Arms against their Country, to become the executioners of their friends and Brethren, or to fall themselves by their Hands.

He has excited domestic insurrections amongst us, and has endeavoured to bring on the inhabitants of our frontiers, the merciless Indian Savages, whose known rule of warfare, is an undistinguished destruction of all ages, sexes and conditions.

In every stage of these Oppressions We have Petitioned for Redress in the most humble terms: Our repeated Petitions have been answered only by repeated injury. A Prince whose character is thus marked by every act which may define a Tyrant, is unfit to be the ruler of a free people.

Nor have We been wanting in attentions to our Brittish brethren. We have warned them from time to time of attempts by their legislature to extend an unwarrantable jurisdiction over us. We have reminded them of the circumstances of our emigration and settlement here. We have appealed to their native justice and magnanimity, and we have conjured them by the ties of our common kindred to disavow these usurpations, which, would inevitably interrupt our connections and correspondence. They too have been deaf to the voice of justice and of consanguinity. We must, therefore, acquiesce in the necessity, which denounces our Separation, and hold them, as we hold the rest of mankind, Enemies in War, in Peace Friends.

We, therefore, the Representatives of the united States of America, in General Congress, Assembled, appealing to the Supreme Judge of the world for the rectitude of our intentions, do, in the Name, and by Authority of the good People of these Colonies, solemnly publish and declare, That these United Colonies are, and of Right ought to be Free and Independent States; that they are Absolved from all Allegiance to the British Crown, and that all political connection between them and the State of Great Britain, is and ought to be totally dissolved; and that as Free and Independent States, they have full Power to levy War, conclude Peace, contract Alliances, establish Commerce, and to do all other Acts and Things which Independent States may of right do. And for the support of this Declaration, with a firm reliance on the protection of divine Providence, we mutually pledge to each other our Lives, our Fortunes and our sacred Honor.

New Hampshire	Josiah Bartlett
	William Whipple
	Matthew Thornton
Massachusetts	John Hancock
	Samuel Adams
	John Adams
	Robert Treat Paine
	Elbridge Gerry
Rhode Island	Stephen Hopkins
	William Ellery
Connecticut	Roger Sherman
	Samuel Huntington
	William Williams
	Oliver Wolcott
New York	William Floyd
	Philip Livingston
	Francis Lewis
	Lewis Morris
New Jersey	Richard Stockton
	John Witherspoon
	Francis Hopkinson
	John Hart
	Abraham Clark
Pennsylvania	Robert Morris
	Benjamin Rush
	Benjamin Franklin
	John Morton
	George Clymer
	James Smith
	George Taylor
	James Wilson
	George Ross
Delaware	Caesar Rodney
	George Read
	Thomas McKean
Maryland	Samuel Chase
	William Paca
	Thomas Stone
	Charles Carroll of Carrollton

Virginia	George Wythe
	Richard Henry Lee
	Thomas Jefferson
	Benjamin Harrison
	Thomas Nelson, Jr.
	Francis Lightfoot Lee
	Carter Braxton
North Carolina	William Hooper
	Joseph Hewes
	John Penn
South Carolina	Edward Rutledge
	Thomas Heyward, Jr.
	Thomas Lynch, Jr.
	Arthur Middleton
Georgia	Button Gwinnett
	Lyman Hall
	George Walton

THE CONSTITUTION
OF THE UNITED STATES

WE THE PEOPLE of the United States, in Order to form a more perfect Union, establish Justice, insure domestic Tranquility, provide for the common defence, promote the general Welfare, and secure the Blessings of Liberty to ourselves and our Posterity, do ordain and establish this Constitution for the United States of America.

Article. I.

Section. 1. All legislative Powers herein granted shall be vested in a Congress of the United States, which shall consist of a Senate and House of Representatives.

Section. 2. The House of Representatives shall be composed of Members chosen every second Year by the People of the several States, and the Electors in each State shall have the Qualifications requisite for Electors of the most numerous Branch of the State Legislature.

No Person shall be a Representative who shall not have attained to the Age of twenty five Years, and been seven Years a Citizen of the United States, and who shall not, when elected, be an Inhabitant of that State in which he shall be chosen.

[Representatives and direct Taxes shall be apportioned among the several States which may be included within this Union, according to their respective Numbers, which shall be determined by adding to the whole Number of free Persons, including those bound to Service for a Term of Years, and excluding Indians not taxed, three fifths of all other Persons.][1] The actual Enumeration shall be made within three Years after the first Meeting of the Congress of the United States, and within every subsequent Term of ten Years, in such Manner as they shall by Law direct. The Number of Representatives shall not exceed one for every thirty Thousand, but each State shall have at Least one Representative; and until such enumeration shall be made, the State of New Hampshire shall be entitled to chuse three, Massachusetts eight, Rhode-Island and Providence Plantations one, Connecticut five, New-York six, New Jersey four, Pennsylvania eight, Delaware one, Maryland six, Virginia ten, North Carolina five, South Carolina five, and Georgia three.

When vacancies happen in the Representation from any State, the Executive Authority thereof shall issue Writs of Election to fill such Vacancies.

The House of Representatives shall chuse their Speaker and other Officers; and shall have the sole Power of Impeachment.

Section. 3. The Senate of the United States shall be composed of

---

1. Changed by section 2 of Amendment XIV

two Senators from each State, [chosen by the Legislature thereof][2] for six Years; and each Senator shall have one Vote.

Immediately after they shall be assembled in Consequence of the first Election, they shall be divided as equally as may be into three Classes. The Seats of the Senators of the first Class shall be vacated at the Expiration of the second Year, of the second Class at the Expiration of the fourth Year, and of the third Class at the Expiration of the sixth Year, so that one third may be chosen every second Year; [and if Vacancies happen by Resignation, or otherwise, during the Recess of the Legislature of any State, the Executive thereof may make temporary Appointments until the next Meeting of the Legislature, which shall then fill such Vacancies.][3]

No Person shall be a Senator who shall not have attained to the Age of thirty Years, and been nine Years a Citizen of the United States, and who shall not, when elected, be an Inhabitant of that State for which he shall be chosen.

The Vice President of the United States shall be President of the Senate, but shall have no Vote, unless they be equally divided.

The Senate shall chuse their other Officers, and also a President pro tempore, in the Absence of the Vice President, or when he shall exercise the Office of President of the United States.

The Senate shall have the sole Power to try all Impeachments. When sitting for that Purpose, they shall be on Oath or Affirmation. When the President of the United States is tried, the Chief Justice shall preside: And no Person shall be convicted without the Concurrence of two thirds of the Members present.

Judgment in Cases of Impeachment shall not extend further than to removal from Office, and disqualification to hold and enjoy any Office of honor, Trust or Profit under the United States: but the Party convicted shall nevertheless be liable and subject to Indictment, Trial, Judgment and Punishment, according to Law.

Section. 4. The Times, Places and Manner of holding Elections for Senators and Representatives, shall be prescribed in each State by the Legislature thereof; but the Congress may at any time by Law make or alter such Regulations, except as to the Places of chusing Senators.

The Congress shall assemble at least once in every Year, and such Meeting shall be [on the first Monday in December,][4] unless they shall by Law appoint a different Day.

Section. 5. Each House shall be the Judge of the Elections, Returns and Qualifications of its own Members, and a Majority of each shall constitute a Quorum to do Business; but a smaller Number may adjourn from

---

2. Changed by Amendment XVII

3. Changed by Amendment XVII

4. Changed by Section 2 of Amendment XX

day to day, and may be authorized to compel the Attendance of absent Members, in such Manner, and under such Penalties as each House may provide.

Each House may determine the Rules of its Proceedings, punish its Members for disorderly Behaviour, and, with the Concurrence of two thirds, expel a Member.

Each House shall keep a Journal of its Proceedings, and from time to time publish the same, excepting such Parts as may in their Judgment require Secrecy; and the Yeas and Nays of the Members of either House on any question shall, at the Desire of one fifth of those Present, be entered on the Journal.

Neither House, during the Session of Congress, shall, without the Consent of the other, adjourn for more than three days, nor to any other Place than that in which the two Houses shall be sitting.

Section. 6. The Senators and Representatives shall receive a Compensation for their Services, to be ascertained by Law, and paid out of the Treasury of the United States. They shall in all Cases, except Treason, Felony and Breach of the Peace, be privileged from Arrest during their Attendance at the Session of their respective Houses, and in going to and returning from the same; and for any Speech or Debate in either House, they shall not be questioned in any other Place.

No Senator or Representative shall, during the Time for which he was elected, be appointed to any civil Office under the Authority of the United States, which shall have been created, or the Emoluments whereof shall have been encreased during such time; and no Person holding any Office under the United States, shall be a Member of either House during his Continuance in Office.

Section. 7. All Bills for raising Revenue shall originate in the House of Representatives; but the Senate may propose or concur with Amendments as on other Bills.

Every Bill which shall have passed the House of Representatives and the Senate, shall, before it become a Law, be presented to the President of the United States: If he approve he shall sign it, but if not he shall return it, with his Objections to that House in which it shall have originated, who shall enter the Objections at large on their Journal, and proceed to reconsider it. If after such Reconsideration two thirds of that House shall agree to pass the Bill, it shall be sent, together with the Objections, to the other House, by which it shall likewise be reconsidered, and if approved by two thirds of that House, it shall become a Law. But in all such Cases the Votes of both Houses shall be determined by yeas and Nays, and the Names of the Persons voting for and against the Bill shall be entered on the Journal of each House respectively. If any Bill shall not be returned by the President within ten Days (Sundays excepted) after it shall have been presented to him, the Same shall be a Law, in like Manner as if he had signed it, unless the Congress by their Adjournment prevent its Return, in which Case it shall not be a Law.

Every Order, Resolution, or Vote to which the Concurrence of the Senate and House of Representatives may be necessary (except on a question of Adjournment) shall be presented to the President of the United States; and before the Same shall take Effect, shall be approved by him, or being disapproved by him, shall be repassed by two thirds of the Senate and House of Representatives, according to the Rules and Limitations prescribed in the Case of a Bill.

Section. 8. The Congress shall have Power To lay and collect Taxes, Duties, Imposts and Excises, to pay the Debts and provide for the common Defence and general Welfare of the United States; but all Duties, Imposts and Excises shall be uniform throughout the United States;

To borrow Money on the credit of the United States;

To regulate Commerce with foreign Nations, and among the several States, and with the Indian Tribes;

To establish an uniform Rule of Naturalization, and uniform Laws on the subject of Bankruptcies throughout the United States;

To coin Money, regulate the Value thereof, and of foreign Coin, and fix the Standard of Weights and Measures;

To provide for the Punishment of counterfeiting the Securities and current Coin of the United States;

To establish Post Offices and post Roads;

To promote the Progress of Science and useful Arts, by securing for limited Times to Authors and Inventors the exclusive Right to their respective Writings and Discoveries;

To constitute Tribunals inferior to the supreme Court;

To define and punish Piracies and Felonies committed on the high Seas, and Offences against the Law of Nations;

To declare War, grant Letters of Marque and Reprisal, and make Rules concerning Captures on Land and Water;

To raise and support Armies, but no Appropriation of Money to that Use shall be for a longer Term than two Years;

To provide and maintain a Navy;

To make Rules for the Government and Regulation of the land and naval Forces;

To provide for calling forth the Militia to execute the Laws of the Union, suppress Insurrections and repel Invasions;

To provide for organizing, arming, and disciplining, the Militia, and for governing such Part of them as may be employed in the Service of the United States, reserving to the States respectively, the Appointment of the Officers, and the Authority of training the Militia according to the discipline prescribed by Congress;

To exercise exclusive Legislation in all Cases whatsoever, over such

District (not exceeding ten Miles square) as may, by Cession of particular States, and the Acceptance of Congress, become the Seat of the Government of the United States, and to exercise like Authority over all Places purchased by the Consent of the Legislature of the State in which the same shall be, for the Erection of Forts, Magazines, Arsenals, dock-yards, and other needful Buildings;—And

To make all Laws which shall be necessary and proper for carrying into Execution the foregoing Powers, and all other Powers vested by this Constitution in the Government of the United States, or in any Department or Officer thereof.

Section. 9. The Migration or Importation of such Persons as any of the States now existing shall think proper to admit, shall not be prohibited by the Congress prior to the Year one thousand eight hundred and eight, but a Tax or duty may be imposed on such Importation, not exceeding ten Dollars for each Person.

The Privilege of the Writ of Habeas Corpus shall not be suspended, unless when in Cases of Rebellion or Invasion the public Safety may require it.

No Bill of Attainder or ex post facto Law shall be passed.

No Capitation, or other direct, Tax shall be laid, [unless in Proportion to the Census or enumeration herein before directed to be taken.][5]

No Tax or Duty shall be laid on Articles exported from any State.

No Preference shall be given by any Regulation of Commerce or Revenue to the Ports of one State over those of another; nor shall Vessels bound to, or from, one State, be obliged to enter, clear, or pay Duties in another.

No Money shall be drawn from the Treasury, but in Consequence of Appropriations made by Law; and a regular Statement and Account of the Receipts and Expenditures of all public Money shall be published from time to time.

No Title of Nobility shall be granted by the United States: And no Person holding any Office of Profit or Trust under them, shall, without the Consent of the Congress, accept of any present, Emolument, Office, or Title, of any kind whatever, from any King, Prince, or foreign State.

Section. 10. No State shall enter into any Treaty, Alliance, or Confederation; grant Letters of Marque and Reprisal; coin Money; emit Bills of Credit; make any Thing but gold and silver Coin a Tender in Payment of Debts; pass any Bill of Attainder, ex post facto Law, or Law impairing the Obligation of Contracts, or grant any Title of Nobility.

No State shall, without the Consent of the Congress, lay any Imposts or Duties on Imports or Exports, except what may be absolutely necessary for executing it's inspection Laws: and the net Produce of all Duties

See Amendment XVI

and Imposts, laid by any State on Imports or Exports, shall be for the Use of the Treasury of the United States; and all such Laws shall be subject to the Revision and Controul of the Congress.

No State shall, without the Consent of Congress, lay any Duty of Tonnage, keep Troops, or Ships of War in time of Peace, enter into any Agreement or Compact with another State, or with a foreign Power, or engage in War, unless actually invaded, or in such imminent Danger as will not admit of delay.

Article. II.

Section. 1. The executive Power shall be vested in a President of the United States of America. He shall hold his Office during the Term of four Years, and, together with the Vice President, chosen for the same Term, be elected, as follows:

Each State shall appoint, in such Manner as the Legislature thereof may direct, a Number of Electors, equal to the whole Number of Senators and Representatives to which the State may be entitled in the Congress: but no Senator or Representative, or Person holding an Office of Trust or Profit under the United States, shall be appointed an Elector.

[The Electors shall meet in their respective States, and vote by Ballot for two Persons, of whom one at least shall not be an Inhabitant of the same State with themselves. And they shall make a List of all the Persons voted for, and of the Number of Votes for each; which List they shall sign and certify, and transmit sealed to the Seat of the Government of the United States, directed to the President of the Senate. The President of the Senate shall, in the Presence of the Senate and House of Representatives, open all the Certificates, and the Votes shall then be counted. The Person having the greatest Number of Votes shall be the President, if such Number be a Majority of the whole Number of Electors appointed; and if there be more than one who have such Majority, and have an equal Number of Votes, then the House of Representatives shall immediately chuse by Ballot one of them for President; and if no Person have a Majority, then from the five highest on the List the said House shall in like Manner chuse the President. But in chusing the President, the Votes shall be taken by States, the Representation from each State having one Vote; A quorum for this purpose shall consist of a Member or Members from two thirds of the States, and a Majority of all the States shall be necessary to a Choice. In every Case, after the Choice of the President, the Person having the greatest Number of Votes of the Electors shall be the Vice President. But if there should remain two or more who have equal Votes, the Senate shall chuse from them by Ballot the Vice President.][6]

The Congress may determine the Time of chusing the Electors, and

6. Changed by Amendment XII

he Day on which they shall give their Votes; which Day shall be the same throughout the United States.

No Person except a natural born Citizen, or a Citizen of the United States, at the time of the Adoption of this Constitution, shall be eligible to the Office of President; neither shall any Person be eligible to that Office who shall not have attained to the Age of thirty five Years, and been fourteen Years a Resident within the United States.

[In Case of the Removal of the President from Office, or of his Death, Resignation, or Inability to discharge the Powers and Duties of the said Office, the Same shall devolve on the Vice President, and the Congress may by Law provide for the Case of Removal, Death, Resignation or Inability, both of the President and Vice President, declaring what Officer shall then act as President, and such Officer shall act accordingly, until the Disability be removed, or a President shall be elected.][7]

The President shall, at stated Times, receive for his Services, a Compensation, which shall neither be increased nor diminished during the Period for which he shall have been elected, and he shall not receive within that Period any other Emolument from the United States, or any of them.

Before he enter on the Execution of his Office, he shall take the following Oath or Affirmation:– "I do solemnly swear (or affirm) that I will faithfully execute the Office of President of the United States, and will to the best of my Ability, preserve, protect and defend the Constitution of the United States."

Section. 2. The President shall be Commander in Chief of the Army and Navy of the United States, and of the Militia of the several States, when called into the actual Service of the United States; he may require the Opinion, in writing, of the principal Officer in each of the executive Departments, upon any Subject relating to the Duties of their respective Offices, and he shall have Power to grant Reprieves and Pardons for Offences against the United States, except in Cases of Impeachment.

He shall have Power, by and with the Advice and Consent of the Senate, to make Treaties, provided two thirds of the Senators present concur; and he shall nominate, and by and with the Advice and Consent of the Senate, shall appoint Ambassadors, other public Ministers and Consuls, Judges of the supreme Court, and all other Officers of the United States, whose Appointments are not herein otherwise provided for, and which shall be established by Law: but the Congress may by Law vest the Appointment of such inferior Officers, as they think proper, in the President alone, in the Courts of Law, or in the Heads of Departments.

The President shall have Power to fill up all Vacancies that may happen during the Recess of the Senate, by granting Commissions which shall expire at the End of their next Session.

Changed by Amendment XXV

Section. 3. He shall from time to time give to the Congress Information of the State of the Union, and recommend to their Consideration such Measures as he shall judge necessary and expedient; he may, on extraordinary Occasions, convene both Houses, or either of them, and in Case of Disagreement between them, with Respect to the Time of Adjournment, he may adjourn them to such Time as he shall think proper; he shall receive Ambassadors and other public Ministers; he shall take Care that the Laws be faithfully executed, and shall Commission all the Officers of the United States.

Section. 4. The President, Vice President and all civil Officers of the United States, shall be removed from Office on Impeachment for, and Conviction of, Treason, Bribery, or other high Crimes and Misdemeanors.

Article III.

Section. 1. The judicial Power of the United States shall be vested in one supreme Court, and in such inferior Courts as the Congress may from time to time ordain and establish. The Judges, both of the supreme and inferior Courts, shall hold their Offices during good Behaviour, and shall, at stated Times, receive for their Services a Compensation, which shall not be diminished during their Continuance in Office.

Section. 2. The judicial Power shall extend to all Cases, in Law and Equity, arising under this Constitution, the Laws of the United States, and Treaties made, or which shall be made, under their Authority;—to all Cases affecting Ambassadors, other public Ministers and Consuls;—to all Cases of admiralty and maritime Jurisdiction;—to Controversies to which the United States shall be a Party;—to Controversies between two or more States;— [between a State and Citizens of another State;—][8] between Citizens of different States;—between Citizens of the same State claiming Lands under Grants of different States, [and between a State, or the Citizens thereof, and foreign States, Citizens or Subjects.][9]

In all Cases affecting Ambassadors, other public Ministers and Consuls, and those in which a State shall be Party, the supreme Court shall have original Jurisdiction. In all the other Cases before mentioned, the supreme Court shall have appellate Jurisdiction, both as to Law and Fact, with such Exceptions, and under such Regulations as the Congress shall make.

The Trial of all Crimes, except in Cases of Impeachment, shall be by Jury; and such Trial shall be held in the State where the said Crimes shall have been committed; but when not committed within any State, the Trial shall be at such Place or Places as the Congress may by Law have directed.

8. Changed by Amendment XI
9. Changed by Amendment XI

Section. 3. Treason against the United States, shall consist only in levying War against them, or in adhering to their Enemies, giving them Aid and Comfort. No Person shall be convicted of Treason unless on the Testimony of two Witnesses to the same overt Act, or on Confession in open Court.

The Congress shall have Power to declare the Punishment of Treason, but no Attainder of Treason shall work Corruption of Blood, or Forfeiture except during the Life of the Person attainted.

Article. IV.

Section. 1. Full Faith and Credit shall be given in each State to the public Acts, Records, and judicial Proceedings of every other State. And the Congress may by general Laws prescribe the Manner in which such Acts, Records and Proceedings shall be proved, and the Effect thereof.

Section. 2. The Citizens of each State shall be entitled to all Privileges and Immunities of Citizens in the several States.

A Person charged in any State with Treason, Felony, or other Crime, who shall flee from Justice, and be found in another State, shall on Demand of the executive Authority of the State from which he fled, be delivered up, to be removed to the State having Jurisdiction of the Crime.

[No Person held to Service or Labour in one State, under the Laws thereof, escaping into another, shall, in Consequence of any Law or Regulation therein, be discharged from such Service or Labour, but shall be delivered up on Claim of the Party to whom such Service or Labour may be due.][10]

Section. 3. New States may be admitted by the Congress into this Union; but no new State shall be formed or erected within the Jurisdiction of any other State; nor any State be formed by the Junction of two or more States, or Parts of States, without the Consent of the Legislatures of the States concerned as well as of the Congress.

The Congress shall have Power to dispose of and make all needful Rules and Regulations respecting the Territory or other Property belonging to the United States; and nothing in this Constitution shall be so construed as to Prejudice any Claims of the United States, or of any particular State.

Section. 4. The United States shall guarantee to every State in this Union a Republican Form of Government, and shall protect each of them against Invasion; and on Application of the Legislature, or of the Executive (when the Legislature cannot be convened), against domestic Violence.

Article. V.

The Congress, whenever two thirds of both Houses shall deem it necessary, shall propose Amendments to this Constitution, or, on the Application of the Legislatures of two thirds of the several States, shall call

---

10. Changed by Amendment XIII

a Convention for proposing Amendments, which, in either Case, shall be valid to all Intents and Purposes, as Part of this Constitution, when ratified by the Legislatures of three fourths of the several States, or by Conventions in three fourths thereof, as the one or the other Mode of Ratification may be proposed by the Congress; Provided that no Amendment which may be made prior to the Year One thousand eight hundred and eight shall in any Manner affect the first and fourth Clauses in the Ninth Section of the first Article; and that no State, without its Consent, shall be deprived of its equal Suffrage in the Senate.

Article. VI.

All Debts contracted and Engagements entered into, before the Adoption of this Constitution, shall be as valid against the United States under this Constitution, as under the Confederation.

This Constitution, and the Laws of the United States which shall be made in Pursuance thereof; and all Treaties made, or which shall be made, under the Authority of the United States, shall be the supreme Law of the Land; and the Judges in every State shall be bound thereby, any Thing in the Constitution or Laws of any State to the Contrary notwithstanding.

The Senators and Representatives before mentioned, and the Members of the several State Legislatures, and all executive and judicial Officers, both of the United States and of the several States, shall be bound by Oath or Affirmation, to support this Constitution; but no religious Test shall ever be required as a Qualification to any Office or public Trust under the United States.

Article. VII.

The Ratification of the Conventions of nine States, shall be sufficient for the Establishment of this Constitution between the States so ratifying the Same.

The Word, "the," being interlined between the seventh and eighth Lines of the first Page, the Word "Thirty" being partly written on an Erazure in the fifteenth Line of the first Page, The Words "is tried" being interlined between the thirty second and thirty third Lines of the first Page and the Word "the" being interlined between the forty third and forty fourth Lines of the second Page.

Done in Convention by the Unanimous Consent of the States present the Seventeenth Day of September in the Year of our Lord one thousand seven hundred and Eighty seven and of the Independence of the United States of America the Twelfth In witness whereof We have hereunto subscribed our Names,

G°. Washington
Presidt and deputy from Virginia

Delaware	Geo: Read
	Gunning Bedford jun
	John Dickinson
	Richard Bassett
	Jaco: Broom
Maryland	James McHenry
	Dan of St Thos. Jenifer
	Danl. Carroll
Virginia	John Blair
	James Madison Jr.
North Carolina	Wm. Blount
	Richd. Dobbs Spaight
	Hu Williamson
South Carolina	J. Rutledge
	Charles Cotesworth Pinckney
	Charles Pinckney
	Pierce Butler
Georgia	William Few
	Abr Baldwin
New Hampshire	John Langdon
	Nicholas Gilman
Massachusetts	Nathaniel Gorham
	Rufus King
Connecticut	Wm. Saml. Johnson
	Roger Sherman
New York	Alexander Hamilton
New Jersey	Wil: Livingston
	David Brearley
	Wm. Paterson
	Jona: Dayton
Pennsylvania	B Franklin
	Thomas Mifflin
	Robt. Morris
	Geo. Clymer
	Thos. FitzSimons
	Jared Ingersoll
	James Wilson
	Gouv Morris

Attest William Jackson Secretary

AMENDMENTS
TO THE CONSTITUTION

The Preamble to The Bill of Rights[11]

Congress of the United States begun and held at the City of New-York, on Wednesday the fourth of March, one thousand seven hundred and eighty nine.

THE Conventions of a number of the States, having at the time of their adopting the Constitution, expressed a desire, in order to prevent misconstruction or abuse of its powers, that further declaratory and restrictive clauses should be added: And as extending the ground of public confidence in the Government, will best ensure the beneficent ends of its institution.

RESOLVED by the Senate and House of Representatives of the United States of America, in Congress assembled, two thirds of both Houses concurring, that the following Articles be proposed to the Legislatures of the several States, as amendments to the Constitution of the United States, all, or any of which Articles, when ratified by three fourths of the said Legislatures, to be valid to all intents and purposes, as part of the said Constitution; viz.

ARTICLES in addition to, and Amendment of the Constitution of the United States of America, proposed by Congress, and ratified by the Legislatures of the several States, pursuant to the fifth Article of the original Constitution.

Amendment I

Congress shall make no law respecting an establishment of religion, or prohibiting the free exercise thereof; or abridging the freedom of speech, or of the press; or the right of the people peaceably to assemble, and to petition the Government for a redress of grievances.

Amendment II

A well regulated Militia being necessary to the security of a free State, the right of the people to keep and bear Arms shall not be infringed.

Amendment III

No Soldier shall, in time of peace be quartered in any house, without the consent of the Owner, nor in time of war, but in a manner to be prescribed by law.

Amendment IV

The right of the people to be secure in their persons, houses, papers, and effects, against unreasonable searches and seizures, shall not be

11. The Bill of Rights (Amendments I - X) was ratified
December 15, 1791.

violated, and no Warrants shall issue, but upon probable cause, supported by Oath or affirmation, and particularly describing the place to be searched, and the persons or things to be seized.

Amendment V

No person shall be held to answer for a capital, or otherwise infamous crime, unless on a presentment or indictment of a Grand Jury, except in cases arising in the land or naval forces, or in the Militia, when in actual service in time of War or public danger; nor shall any person be subject for the same offence to be twice put in jeopardy of life or limb; nor shall be compelled in any criminal case to be a witness against himself, nor be deprived of life, liberty, or property, without due process of law; nor shall private property be taken for public use, without just compensation.

Amendment VI

In all criminal prosecutions, the accused shall enjoy the right to a speedy and public trial, by an impartial jury of the State and district wherein the crime shall have been committed, which district shall have been previously ascertained by law, and to be informed of the nature and cause of the accusation; to be confronted with the witnesses against him; to have compulsory process for obtaining witnesses in his favor, and to have the Assistance of Counsel for his defence.

Amendment VII

In suits at common law, where the value in controversy shall exceed twenty dollars, the right of trial by jury shall be preserved, and no fact tried by a jury, shall be otherwise reexamined in any Court of the United States, than according to the rules of the common law.

Amendment VIII

Excessive bail shall not be required, nor excessive fines imposed, nor cruel and unusual punishments inflicted.

Amendment IX

The enumeration in the Constitution, of certain rights, shall not be construed to deny or disparage others retained by the people.

Amendment X

The powers not delegated to the United States by the Constitution, nor prohibited by it to the States, are reserved to the States respectively, or to the people.

Amendment XI[12]

The Judicial power of the United States shall not be construed to extend to any suit in law or equity, commenced or prosecuted against one of the United States by Citizens of another State, or by Citizens or Subjects of any Foreign State.

12. Ratified February 7, 1795

Amendment XII[13]

The Electors shall meet in their respective states and vote by ballot for President and Vice-President, one of whom, at least, shall not be an inhabitant of the same state with themselves; they shall name in their ballots the person voted for as President, and in distinct ballots the person voted for as Vice-President, and they shall make distinct lists of all persons voted for as President, and of all persons voted for as Vice-President, and of the number of votes for each, which lists they shall sign and certify, and transmit sealed to the seat of the government of the United States, directed to the President of the Senate; — the President of the Senate shall, in the presence of the Senate and House of Representatives, open all the certificates and the votes shall then be counted; — The person having the greatest number of votes for President, shall be the President, if such number be a majority of the whole number of Electors appointed; and if no person have such majority, then from the persons having the highest numbers not exceeding three on the list of those voted for as President, the House of Representatives shall choose immediately, by ballot, the President. But in choosing the President, the votes shall be taken by states, the representation from each state having one vote; a quorum for this purpose shall consist of a member or members from two-thirds of the states, and a majority of all the states shall be necessary to a choice. [And if the House of Representatives shall not choose a President whenever the right of choice shall devolve upon them, before the fourth day of March next following, then the Vice-President shall act as President, as in case of the death or other constitutional disability of the President. —][14] The person having the greatest number of votes as Vice-President, shall be the Vice-President, if such number be a majority of the whole number of Electors appointed, and if no person have a majority, then from the two highest numbers on the list, the Senate shall choose the Vice-President; a quorum for the purpose shall consist of two-thirds of the whole number of Senators, and a majority of the whole number shall be necessary to a choice. But no person constitutionally ineligible to the office of President shall be eligible to that of Vice-President of the United States.

Amendment XIII[15]

Section 1. Neither slavery nor involuntary servitude, except as a punishment for crime whereof the party shall have been duly convicted, shall exist within the United States, or any place subject to their jurisdiction.

Section 2. Congress shall have power to enforce this article by appropriate legislation.

---

13. Ratified June 15, 1804

14. Superseded by section 3 of Amendment XX

15. Ratified December 6, 1865

Amendment XIV[16]

Section 1. All persons born or naturalized in the United States, and subject to the jurisdiction thereof, are citizens of the United States and of the State wherein they reside. No State shall make or enforce any law which shall abridge the privileges or immunities of citizens of the United States; nor shall any State deprive any person of life, liberty, or property, without due process of law; nor deny to any person within its jurisdiction the equal protection of the laws.

Section 2. Representatives shall be apportioned among the several States according to their respective numbers, counting the whole number of persons in each State, excluding Indians not taxed. But when the right to vote at any election for the choice of electors for President and Vice-President of the United States, Representatives in Congress, the Executive and Judicial officers of a State, or the members of the Legislature thereof, is denied to any of the male inhabitants of such State, being twenty-one years of age, and citizens of the United States, or in any way abridged, except for participation in rebellion, or other crime, the basis of representation therein shall be reduced in the proportion which the number of such male citizens shall bear to the whole number of male citizens twenty-one years of age in such State.

Section 3. No person shall be a Senator or Representative in Congress, or elector of President and Vice-President, or hold any office, civil or military, under the United States, or under any State, who, having previously taken an oath, as a member of Congress, or as an officer of the United States, or as a member of any State legislature, or as an executive or judicial officer of any State, to support the Constitution of the United States, shall have engaged in insurrection or rebellion against the same, or given aid or comfort to the enemies thereof. But Congress may by a vote of two-thirds of each House, remove such disability.

Section 4. The validity of the public debt of the United States, authorized by law, including debts incurred for payment of pensions and bounties for services in suppressing insurrection or rebellion, shall not be questioned. But neither the United States nor any State shall assume or pay any debt or obligation incurred in aid of insurrection or rebellion against the United States, or any claim for the loss or emancipation of any slave; but all such debts, obligations and claims shall be held illegal and void.

Section 5. The Congress shall have the power to enforce, by appropriate legislation, the provisions of this article.

Amendment XV[17]

Section 1. The right of citizens of the United States to vote shall not be denied or abridged by the United States or by any State on ac-

16. Ratified July 9, 1868

17. Ratified February 3, 1870

count of race, color, or previous condition of servitude—

Section 2. The Congress shall have the power to enforce this article by appropriate legislation.

Amendment XVI[18]

The Congress shall have power to lay and collect taxes on incomes, from whatever source derived, without apportionment among the several States, and without regard to any census or enumeration.

Amendment XVII[19]

The Senate of the United States shall be composed of two Senators from each State, elected by the people thereof, for six years; and each Senator shall have one vote. The electors in each State shall have the qualifications requisite for electors of the most numerous branch of the State legislatures.

When vacancies happen in the representation of any State in the Senate, the executive authority of such State shall issue writs of election to fill such vacancies: Provided, That the legislature of any State may empower the executive thereof to make temporary appointments until the people fill the vacancies by election as the legislature may direct.

This amendment shall not be so construed as to affect the election or term of any Senator chosen before it becomes valid as part of the Constitution.

Amendment XVIII[20]

[**Section 1.** After one year from the ratification of this article the manufacture, sale, or transportation of intoxicating liquors within, the importation thereof into, or the exportation thereof from the United States and all territory subject to the jurisdiction thereof for beverage purposes is hereby prohibited.

Section 2. The Congress and the several States shall have concurrent power to enforce this article by appropriate legislation.

Section 3. This article shall be inoperative unless it shall have been ratified as an amendment to the Constitution by the legislatures of the several States, as provided in the Constitution, within seven years from the date of the submission hereof to the States by the Congress.]

Amendment XIX[21]

The right of citizens of the United States to vote shall not be denied or abridged by the United States or by any State on account of sex.

Congress shall have power to enforce this article by appropriate legislation.

---

18. Ratified February 3, 1913

19. Ratified April 8, 1913

20. Amendment XVIII was ratified January 16, 1919. It was repealed by Amendment XXI, December 5, 1933.

21. Ratified August 18, 1920

Amendment XX[22]

Section 1. The terms of the President and the Vice President shall end at noon on the 20th day of January, and the terms of Senators and Representatives at noon on the 3d day of January, of the years in which such terms would have ended if this article had not been ratified; and the terms of their successors shall then begin.

Section 2. The Congress shall assemble at least once in every year, and such meeting shall begin at noon on the 3d day of January, unless they shall by law appoint a different day.

Section 3. If, at the time fixed for the beginning of the term of the President, the President elect shall have died, the Vice President elect shall become President. If a President shall not have been chosen before the time fixed for the beginning of his term, or if the President elect shall have failed to qualify, then the Vice President elect shall act as President until a President shall have qualified; and the Congress may by law provide for the case wherein neither a President elect nor a Vice President shall have qualified, declaring who shall then act as President, or the manner in which one who is to act shall be selected, and such person shall act accordingly until a President or Vice President shall have qualified.

Section 4. The Congress may by law provide for the case of the death of any of the persons from whom the House of Representatives may choose a President whenever the right of choice shall have devolved upon them, and for the case of the death of any of the persons from whom the Senate may choose a Vice President whenever the right of choice shall have devolved upon them.

Section 5. Sections 1 and 2 shall take effect on the 15th day of October following the ratification of this article.

Section 6. This article shall be inoperative unless it shall have been ratified as an amendment to the Constitution by the legislatures of three-fourths of the several States within seven years from the date of its submission.

Amendment XXI[23]

Section 1. The eighteenth article of amendment to the Constitution of the United States is hereby repealed.

Section 2. The transportation or importation into any State, Territory, or Possession of the United States for delivery or use therein of intoxicating liquors, in violation of the laws thereof, is hereby prohibited.

Section 3. This article shall be inoperative unless it shall have been ratified as an amendment to the Constitution by conventions in the several States, as provided in the Constitution, within seven years from the date of the submission hereof to the States by the Congress.

---

2. Ratified January 23, 1933

3. Ratified December 5, 1933

Amendment XXII[24]

Section 1. No person shall be elected to the office of the President more than twice, and no person who has held the office of President, or acted as President, for more than two years of a term to which some other person was elected President shall be elected to the office of President more than once. But this Article shall not apply to any person holding the office of President when this Article was proposed by Congress, and shall not prevent any person who may be holding the office of President, or acting as President, during the term within which this Article become operative from holding the office of President or acting as President during the remainder of such term.

Section 2. This article shall be inoperative unless it shall have been ratified as an amendment to the Constitution by the legislatures of three-fourths of the several States within seven years from the date of its submission to the States by the Congress.

Amendment XXIII[25]

Section 1. The District constituting the seat of Government of the United States shall appoint in such manner as Congress may direct:

A number of electors of President and Vice President equal to the whole number of Senators and Representatives in Congress to which the District would be entitled if it were a State, but in no event more than the least populous State; they shall be in addition to those appointed by the States, but they shall be considered, for the purposes of the election of President and Vice President, to be electors appointed by a State; and they shall meet in the District and perform such duties as provided by the twelfth article of amendment.

Section 2. The Congress shall have power to enforce this article by appropriate legislation.

Amendment XXIV[26]

Section 1. The right of citizens of the United States to vote in any primary or other election for President or Vice President, for elector for President or Vice President, or for Senator or Representative in Congress, shall not be denied or abridged by the United States or any State by reason of failure to pay poll tax or other tax.

Section 2. The Congress shall have power to enforce this article by appropriate legislation.

Amendment XXV[27]

Section 1. In case of the removal of the President from office or of his death or resignation, the Vice President shall become President

---

24. Ratified February 27, 1951

25. Ratified March 29, 1961

26. Ratified January 23, 1964

27. Ratified February 10, 1967

Section 2. Whenever there is a vacancy in the office of the Vice President, the President shall nominate a Vice President who shall take office upon confirmation by a majority vote of both Houses of Congress.

Section 3. Whenever the President transmits to the President pro tempore of the Senate and the Speaker of the House of Representatives his written declaration that he is unable to discharge the powers and duties of his office, and until he transmits to them a written declaration to the contrary, such powers and duties shall be discharged by the Vice President as Acting President.

Section 4. Whenever the Vice President and a majority of either the principal officers of the executive departments or of such other body as Congress may by law provide, transmit to the President pro tempore of the Senate and the Speaker of the House of Representatives their written declaration that the President is unable to discharge the powers and duties of his office, the Vice President shall immediately assume the powers and duties of the office as Acting President.

Thereafter, when the President transmits to the President pro tempore of the Senate and the Speaker of the House of Representatives his written declaration that no inability exists, he shall resume the powers and duties of his office unless the Vice President and a majority of either the principal officers of the executive department or of such other body as Congress may by law provide, transmit within four days to the President pro tempore of the Senate and the Speaker of the House of Representatives their written declaration that the President is unable to discharge the powers and duties of his office. Thereupon Congress shall decide the issue, assembling within forty-eight hours for that purpose if not in session. If the Congress, within twenty-one days after receipt of the latter written declaration, or, if Congress is not in session, within twenty-one days after Congress is required to assemble, determines by two-thirds vote of both Houses that the President is unable to discharge the powers and duties of his office, the Vice President shall continue to discharge the same as Acting President; otherwise, the President shall resume the powers and duties of his office.

Amendment XXVI[28]

Section 1. The right of citizens of the United States, who are eighteen years of age or older, to vote shall not be denied or abridged by the United States or by any State on account of age.

Section 2. The Congress shall have power to enforce this article by appropriate legislation.

Amendment XXVII[29]

No law, varying the compensation for the services of the Senators and Representatives, shall take effect, until an election of representatives shall have intervened.

---

28. Ratified July 1, 1971

29. Ratified May 7, 1992

OUR SACRED HONOR:
"TO SUPPORT AND DEFEND"

MARK ALEXANDER
PUBLISHER, PATRIOTPOST.US

"Of all the dispositions and habits which lead to political prosperity,
Religion and morality are indispensible supports. In vain would that
man claim the tribute of Patriotism who should labor to subvert these
great Pillars of human happiness — these firmest props of the duties
of men and citizens. ... Let it simply be asked where is the security for
property, for reputation, for life, if the sense of religious obligation
desert the oaths..." —President George Washington (1796)

In 1776, an extraordinary group of men signed a document that
affirmed their unalienable right to "life, liberty, and the pursuit of happiness" as "endowed by their Creator." By attaching their signatures
to our great Declaration of Independence, they, in effect, were signing
their death warrants in defense of Essential Liberty.

Indeed, the last line of our Declaration reads, "For the support
of this declaration, with a firm reliance on the protection of Divine
Providence, we mutually pledge to each other our lives, our fortunes
and our sacred honor."

These men, and their countrymen and women, were the first generation of American Patriots, and they had chosen "the animating contest
for freedom," as Samuel Adams put it, rather than "the tranquility of
servitude." Indeed, they were willing to die for the cause of Liberty.

A decade later, Liberty having been won at great cost, our Founders further codified their independence and interdependence by instituting yet another historic document, the United States Constitution.

Our Constitution, as written and ratified, stipulates in its preamble
that it is ordained and established by the people to "secure the
Blessings of Liberty to ourselves and our Posterity." To that end, it
established a Republic, not a popular democracy, which is to say that
it affirmed the primacy of Rule of Law over rule of men.

Accordingly, the first order of business for those we elect to
national office is that they be bound by oath to "preserve, protect and
defend" the Constitution under which they were duly elected.

For those elected to the presidency, Article II, Section 1, specifies:
"Before he enter on the Execution of his Office, he shall take the
following Oath or Affirmation: 'I do solemnly swear (or affirm) that
I will faithfully execute the Office of President of the United States,
and will to the best of my Ability, preserve, protect and defend the
Constitution of the United States.'"

On April 30th, 1789, our nation's first Commander in Chief, George Washington, took the presidential oath of office with his hand on a Bible opened to the book of Deuteronomy, Chapter 28. He ended his oath with "So help me God," which was soon thereafter added to military oaths for officers by Act of Congress.

Later that day, in his First Inaugural Address, President Washington said: "It would be peculiarly improper to omit, in this first official act, my fervent supplications to that Almighty Being who rules over the universe, who presides in the councils of nations, and whose providential aids can supply every human defect." Such was the conduct of his administration.

In his Farewell Address of September 19th, 1796, Washington concluded with these words: "Of all the dispositions and habits which lead to political prosperity, Religion and morality are indispensable supports. In vain would that man claim the tribute of Patriotism, who should labor to subvert these great Pillars of human happiness, these firmest props of the duties of man and citizens. ... Let it be simply asked, where is the security for property, for reputation, for life, if the sense of religious obligation desert the oaths, which are the instruments of investigation in Courts of Justice? And let us with caution indulge the supposition, that morality can be maintained without religion. Whatever may be conceded to the influence of refined education on minds of peculiar structure, reason and experience both forbid us to expect, that national morality can prevail in exclusion of religious principle."

Regarding the Presidential Oath of Office, Justice Joseph Story wrote: "The duty imposed upon him to take care, that the laws be faithfully executed, follows out the strong injunctions of his oath of office, that he will 'preserve, protect, and defend the constitution.' The great object of the executive department is to accomplish this purpose." He wrote further that if the president does not honor his oath, his office "will be utterly worthless for ... the protection of rights; for the happiness, or good order, or safety of the people."

In addition to the Constitution's oath mandate for presidents, Article VI, Clause 3 specifies: "The Senators and Representatives before mentioned, and the Members of the several State Legislatures, and all executive and judicial Officers, both of the United States and of the several States, shall be bound by Oath or Affirmation, to support this Constitution..."

Commissioned officers and enlisted military personnel are also required by statute (Section 3331, Title 5 and 10 U.S.C. § 502, respectively) to "solemnly swear, that I will support and defend the Constitution of the United States against all enemies, foreign and domestic; that I will bear true faith and allegiance to the same..." Commissioned officers (O-1 through O-10, and W-2 through W-5 [chief warrant officers]) receive commissions under the authority of the President with the advice and consent of the Senate. Warrant officers (WO-1) receive their warrant under the authority of their respective service secretary.

Notably, the officer's oath doesn't include any language about following orders, but the enlisted oath does: "I will obey the orders of the President of the United States and the orders of the officers appointed over me, according to regulations and the Uniform Code of Military Justice." However, the UCMJ clearly establishes that enlisted personnel are bound to obey only "lawful orders." The "I was only following orders" defense has been insufficient since first being tested in 1799.

National Guard officers and enlisted personnel "solemnly swear (or affirm)" the following oath: "that I will support and defend the Constitution of the United States and the Constitution of the State (Commonwealth, District, Territory) of (…) against all enemies, foreign and domestic; that I will bear true faith and allegiance to the same; that I will obey the orders of the President of the United States and the Governor of the State (Commonwealth, District, Territory) of (…)." The parameters of "lawful orders" also apply to the Guard oaths.

Here we should note that all of these oaths mandate the preservation, protection, support and defense of our Constitution as ratified, not as modified or misinterpreted by activist judges under the auspices of a "living constitution." Indeed, this is precisely what Jefferson had in mind when he foretold of "the despotic branch."

Generations of American Patriots have honorably supported and defended our Constitution with their blood and their lives. But George Washington warned, "Guard against the impostures of pretended patriotism."

At their core, the words "American Patriot" have their lineage with those who fought for American independence and established our constitutional republic. That lineage, in turn, has been passed down through our history by those who have been entrusted "to support and defend" our Constitution.

In 1775, John Adams wrote to his wife, Abigail, "A Constitution of Government once changed from Freedom, can never be restored. Liberty, once lost, is lost forever."

In 1816, Thomas Jefferson wrote to Charles Yancey, "If a nation expects to be ignorant and free … it expects what never was and never will be."

Indeed.

I have taken my oaths nine times in the service of my country. But I did not have to take an oath to understand my obligations as a citizen "to support and defend" our Constitution. Further, I also note that all duly administered oaths are binding indefinitely — there is no duration specified or defined. Thus, we are bound by our oaths until death do us part.

Semper Vigilans Fortis Paratus et Fidelis
Pro Deo et Libertate — 1776

Mark Alexander
Publisher of *The Patriot Post*

REAFFIRM YOUR OATH
"TO SUPPORT AND DEFEND"

With a full understanding of the authority of the United States Constitution and the Rule of Law it enshrines, reaffirm your oath to "support and defend" our Constitution "against all enemies, foreign and domestic."

If you have previously taken an oath to our Constitution and you remain steadfast in your pledge to "bear true faith and allegiance to the same," reaffirm your commitment by your signature:

_____ *Signature*

Oath taken as Military
☐ *Officer or* ☐ *Enlisted*

Oath taken as Civilian
☐ *Elected or* ☐ *Civil Servant or* ☐ *Public Servant*

Year of Initial Oath: _____

Having reaffirmed your oath, forever stand ready to abide by it when duty calls, and enlist others to do the same.

OATH OF ALLEGIANCE
TO SUPPORT AND DEFEND
THE UNITED STATES
CONSTITUTION

I, _____ (Printed Name) do solemnly swear (or affirm), that I will support and defend the Constitution of the United States against all enemies, foreign and domestic; that I will bear true faith and allegiance to the same, that I take this obligation freely, without any mental reservation or purpose of evasion; So help me God."

_____ *Signature*

Administered by: _____

Affirmed on this _____ *Day of* _____ *in the Year* _____

ESSENTIAL CHRONOLOGY

December 16, 1773: Boston Tea Party

June 14, 1775: Congress establishes the Continental Army

July 6, 1775: Congress issues Declaration of the Cause and Necessity of Taking Up Arms

April 19, 1775: A British attack at Lexington, Massachusetts starts the War of Independence

October 13, 1775: Congress establishes the Continental Navy

November 10, 1775: Congress establishes the Marine Corps

July 4, 1776: Congress adopts Declaration of Independence

November 15, 1777: The Articles of Confederation become effective

October 19, 1781: Cornwallis surrenders at Yorktown, Virginia, ending British military action

September 3, 1783: Great Britain signs Treaty of Paris, recognizing America's independence

May 25, 1787: The Constitutional Convention opens in Philadelphia with quorum of seven states to discuss revising the Articles of Confederation

September 17, 1787: All 12 state delegations approve the Constitution. Of the 42 delegates present, 39 sign it and the Convention formally adjourns

June 21, 1788: The Constitution becomes effective for the ratifying states when New Hampshire is the ninth state to ratify it

March 4, 1789: The first Congress under the Constitution convenes in New York City

April 30, 1789: George Washington is inaugurated as the first president of the United States

June 8, 1789: James Madison introduces proposed Bill of Rights in the House of Representatives

September 24, 1789: Congress establishes a Supreme Court, 13 district courts, three ad hoc circuit courts, and the position of Attorney General

September 25, 1789: Congress approves 12 constitutional amendments and sends them to the states for ratification

February 2, 1790: Supreme Court convenes for the first time

August 4, 1790: Congress establishes the U.S. Coast Guard

December 15, 1791: Virginia ratifies the Bill of Rights, and 10 of the 12 proposed amendments become part of the U.S. Constitution

May 30, 1868: First Memorial Day

September 18, 1947: Congress establishes the U.S. Air Force

May 21, 1949: Armed Forces Day

November 11, 1954: First Veterans Day (Armistice Day)

Essential Liberty Resources

These, and many other resources are available online at
www.essentialliberty.us/document/

The Code of Hammurabi (ca. 1727-1680 BC)
The Ten Commandments (ca. 1447 BC)
The Constitutions of Clarendon (1164)
The Magna Carta (June 15, 1215)
The Declaration of Arbroath (1320)
Privileges Granted Christopher Columbus (1492)
Charter to Sir Walter Raleigh (March 25, 1584)
Colonial Charters (1606-1732)
Mayflower Compact (November 11, 1620)
Surrender of the Great Charter of New England (1635)
Confederation of the United Colonies (May 19, 1643)
The First Thanksgiving Proclamation (1676)
English Bill of Rights (1689)
John Locke: The Second Treatise of Government (1689)
Resolutions of the Stamp Act (1765)
Anonymous Account of the Boston Massacre (March 5, 1770)
Declaration of the First Continental Congress (October 14, 1774)
Give Me Liberty or Give Me Death! (March 23, 1775)
Samuel Adams on American Independence (August 1, 1776)
Common Sense – Thomas Paine (1776)
The Rights of Man – Thomas Paine (1792)
State Constitutions (1776-1778)
The Federalist Papers (1787)
The Anti-Federalist Papers (1787)

SUPPORT THE
ESSENTIAL LIBERTY PROJECT

The mission of the Essential Liberty Project is to support the restoration of constitutional integrity and Rule of Law. Part of that mission is a critical and timely educational initiative to distribute millions of Essential Liberty pocket reference guides.

As a primer on liberty, "endowed by [our] Creator" and codified by our Founders in the Declaration of Independence and the U.S. Constitution, these guides have a proven record as an essential resource for Patriots of all ages.

Join the ranks of Patriots advancing our legacy of liberty by purchasing and/or sponsoring these guides for bulk distribution to military and public service personnel, promotion and advancement ceremonies, students, grassroots organizations, civic events, club or association meetings, Tea Parties, etc.

Support Essential Liberty today!

For more information, or to
Support the Essential Liberty Project online:
EssentialLiberty.US

Support the Essential Liberty Project by mail:
Essential Liberty Project
PO Box 407
Chattanooga, Tennessee 37401 USA
(Make checks payable to "Essential Liberty Project")

NOTES